T0310641

Mastering GitHub Pages

Mastering Computer Science
Series Editor: Sufyan bin Uzayr

Mastering GitHub Pages: A Beginner's Guide
Sumanna Kaul and Shahryar Raz

Mastering Unity: A Beginner's Guide
Divya Sachdeva and Aruqqa Khateib

Mastering Unreal Engine: A Beginner's Guide
Divya Sachdeva and Aruqqa Khateib

Mastering Java: A Beginner's Guide
Divya Sachdeva and Natalya Ustukpayeva

Mastering Python for Web: A Beginner's Guide
Mathew Rooney and Madina Karybzhanova

Mastering MySQL for Web: A Beginner's Guide
Mathew Rooney and Madina Karybzhanova

For more information about this series, please visit: https://www.routledge.com/Mastering-Computer-Science/book-series/MCS

The "Mastering Computer Science" series of books are authored by the Zeba Academy team members, led by Sufyan bin Uzayr.

Zeba Academy is an EdTech venture that develops courses and content for learners primarily in STEM fields, and offers education consulting to Universities and Institutions worldwide. For more info, please visit https://zeba.academy

Mastering GitHub Pages

A Beginner's Guide

Edited by Sufyan bin Uzayr

CRC Press
Taylor & Francis Group
Boca Raton London New York

CRC Press is an imprint of the
Taylor & Francis Group, an **informa** business

First edition published 2022
by CRC Press

6000 Broken Sound Parkway NW, Suite 300, Boca Raton, FL 33487-2742

and by CRC Press
2 Park Square, Milton Park, Abingdon, Oxon, OX14 4RN

CRC Press is an imprint of Taylor & Francis Group, LLC

ISBN: 9781032149837 (hbk)
ISBN: 9781032149783 (pbk)
ISBN: 9781003242055 (ebk)

DOI: 10.1201/9781003242055

Typeset in Minion
KnowledgeWorks Global Ltd.

Contents

About the Editor

Sufyan bin Uzayr is a writer, coder, and entrepreneur with more than a decade of experience in the industry. He has authored several books in the past, pertaining to a diverse range of topics, ranging from History to Computers/IT.

Sufyan is the Director of Parakozm, a multinational IT company specializing in EdTech solutions. He also runs Zeba Academy, an online learning and teaching vertical with a focus on STEM fields.

Sufyan specializes in a wide variety of technologies, such as JavaScript, Dart, WordPress, Drupal, Linux, and Python. He holds multiple degrees, including ones in Management, IT, Literature, and Political Science.

Sufyan is a digital nomad, dividing his time between four countries. He has lived and taught in universities and educational institutions around the globe. Sufyan takes a keen interest in technology, politics, literature, history, and sports, and in his spare time, he enjoys teaching coding and English to young students.

Learn more at sufyanism.com.

CHAPTER 1

Introduction to Git and GitHub

IN THIS CHAPTER

- ➤ What is Git

- ➤ What is Version Control

- ➤ What is GitHub

- ➤ Major Features and Advantages

- ➤ How do GitHub repos work

WHAT IS GIT

Git is generally defined as an Open-Source Distributed VCS (DVCS). We should be familiar with what the word open source means; it is used so that we can denote the

DOI: 10.1201/9781003242055-1

software, in which initial source code is made freely available by the developers and could also be redistributed as well as modified. Now, we are left with the term "Distributed VCS." For better comprehension, let's break this phrase down and go into a word-by-word explanation of the key terms used here. But before that, let's expand upon the acronym we used. VCS is a short form that stands for Version Control System. The primary role of a control system is that of a content tracker. So, Git is mostly used to store content, well actually code, due to the other features it provides its users with. What then is a VCS? A VCS constitutes a software system that will track the history of the changes you make to a file/code so that you can always revert to an earlier version of the main code line. The code is undergoing development and needless to say and is changing all the time. Additionally, hundreds, sometimes even thousands, of developers are sometimes working on the same code simultaneously. This is known as parallel development. Git and other versions of VCSs are able to record the changes being made by all of them, apart from providing features like branches and merges. And what is a DVCS? Git also has a remote repository that gets stored in a server as well as a local repository stored in the computer of every developer who is working on the project. This also means that our code is present not only just in the central server but also along with every developer in their personal systems. Git becomes a "distributed" VCS, just because of this feature. The main code is not the property of any particular center but is distributed across PCs by making use of remote as well as a local repository.

But why exactly are the software development teams and organizations looking for something like Git? Because real-life projects often tend to have multiple coders and developers working on them simultaneously. A VCS, via keeping track of various changesets, will be ensuring that there are no conflicts between coders as far as their respective codes are concerned, particularly due to the provision of tools like pushing and pulling to update latest changes, thus smoothing out the process of merging changes. In addition, the requirements of projects could also change frequently. There might also be a need to revert to an older version of code to solve a pertinent problem that was present in and exemplified by that particular version. A VCS, through creating snapshots, should allow us to clone older versions of the code and work on them all over again, if that is what we need to do. Lastly, most projects contain a multitude of issues being resolved by a huge number of developers simultaneously. This sort of a workflow is only possible through the system of branches. If you are used to working on centralized VCSs, you are bound to find working on Git significantly different. A few crucial pointers to remember about Git:

- Its branches are cheap as well as lightweight, so you should easily be able to have many of them.

- In order to be able to store changes, Git makes use of the Secure Hash Algorithm (SHA), whose primary purpose is to compress the text files, consequently making Git an excellent VCS for purposes of software programming, but not effective in case of binary files like images as well as videos.

- It is fairly easy to connect Git repositories with each other. So, you should be able to work on your local machine and subsequently also connect it to a shared repository. In that way, you should be able to push as well as pull changes into a repository, making the process of collaboration incredibly convenient.

Why Should We Use Git?

Version control, these days, is absolutely indispensable because not using it gives a fair opportunity to the risk of losing your work. Git allows you to make a "commit," i.e., basically saving a point as often as you wish to do so. You are also allowed to go revisit the older commits that you made. This will take a lot of pressure off of you while you are coding. So, you need to commit early and as often as possible, and you will never have to experience that horrifying feeling of overwriting or losing the changes you worked on for hours and hours. Of course, there are many kinds of VCSs available in the market. But if you use Git, you will be rendered with some specific benefits:

- **Speed:** As mentioned above, Git makes use of SHA compression, making it significantly faster than its peers. Additionally, most of the work to be done in the software is local and can be done offline, further enhancing its speed, which is already much higher than its fellow VCSs.

- **Merge conflicts:** Git is adept at handling merge conflicts, which means that it is perfectly okay for many people to work on the same file simultaneously. This leads to the opening up of the world of development in a manner that is simply not possible as far as the case of centralized version control is concerned. You will be able to have access to the entire project, and if you happen to be working on a branch, you are allowed to do whatever you need to do in order to be sure that your changes are perfectly safe.

- **Cheap branches:** As mentioned earlier, Git branches offer a tremendous amount of flexibility as well as opportunities for collaboration with the developers. Via the use of branches, developers are allowed to make their changes in a safe space or experiment inside a safe sandbox. How? Because a mediocre changeset might not pass the review and, subsequently, might not even be merged into the main code line. In absence of branches, such a robust system of review and iteration would simply not be possible.

- **Easy RollBack:** If you were working long hours, and ended up making a mistake, there is absolutely no need to panic. Even though commits themselves are immutable, i.e., they cannot be changed, and you are totally permitted to create new replacement commits that will revert the changes you made in the first place. Additionally, you could also roll back your branch pointer to the commit with no errors, effectively undoing any mistake you might have ended up making. The benefits of this facility cannot be overemphasized. The developers are embedded in a safer environment for both the code and the project at large. Furthermore, developers can be braver with their experiments, with the assurance that in case they mess up, Git will always have their back.

Installation

Before being able to use Git, you would obviously need to make it available in your system. If it has already been installed, update to the latest version nevertheless. The installation can be conducted via a package, another installer, or the downloading as well as the compilation of the mandated code.

Before you start using Git, it is imperative that you make it available on your computer. Even if it's already installed, it's probably a good idea to update to the latest version. You could either install it as a package or via another installer, or download the source code and compile it yourself.

It is fairly easy to install Git on most operating systems (OSs) like Mac, Linux, Windows, etc. In fact, if you are working on a Mac or a Linux system, Git is probably already installed on your machine by default.

Now, we will look at the stepwise processes for a number of affiliated functions pertaining to the installation of Git.

- **Check for Git:** To check if your system has pre-installed Git, you shall have to open up your terminal application.

To make sure if you already have Git installed, open up your terminal application.

- For Mac, find the command prompt application known as "Terminal."

- For Windows, find the Windows command prompt, also known as Git Bash.

On opening the terminal application, type "git version." The output should be able to tell you which version of Git has been installed in your system, or it will let you know that git is a foreign, unknown, or invalid command for it. If you get the latter remarks, you will have to install Git manually into your system.

GitHub Desktop

If you simply install GitHub desktop within your system, you should also be able to get the newest version of Git if you do not have it already. GitHub Desktop will bestow your system with the command-line version of Git along-side a robust Graphical User Interface (GUI). Irrespective of whether Git has been installed in your system or not, GitHub desktop should be able to offer you a simple as well as an effective collaboration tool for Git.

Git on Windows

- Start out by navigating to the latest Git to download and acquire the latest version of Git for Windows installer.

- Once your installer has been initialized, make sure that you follow the provided instructions on the Git setup Wizard screen until your installation takes place.

- Then, open up the Windows command prompt, or Git Bash, if happened to have selected to not use the Git Windows Command Prompt, while you were getting your Git installed.

- Type git version to prompt the verification that Git was installed. Do remember that git-scm is a highly popular as well as recommended resource for you to download Git for your Windows. One advantage of downloading Git from git-scm is that your download will be able to automatically start with the latest version of Git along with the suggested command prompt, Git Bash. The download source will be the same Git for Windows installer that we referred to earlier in this section.

Install Git on Mac

Most versions of MacOSs have their Git pre-installed, and the same can be activated in the terminal window through the command git version. However, if your Mac does not have Git for whatever reason, you should be able to download it using either of the two methods given below:

Installing Git Using an Installer

- Find the latest MacOS Git installer and download it.

- Once the installer has been initiated, follow the provided instructions until the installation is done.

- Now, open the command prompt terminal and type the command git version to verify that your Git was installed.

Installing Git Using Homebrew

Homebrew is a well-known package manager that is used for MacOSs.

If you already have Homebrew within your system, following the provided steps should be able to install Git on your system:

- First, open a terminal window to make sure that you use the command brew install git in order to be able to install Git.

- Verify your installation by using the command git version once the command output has been completed.

Installing Git on Linux

If you go into the historical background of the creation of Git, you will be surprised to know that Linux was the operating system Git was originally developed to version for. So, it certainly doesn't baffle one that the Git software is easy to configure on Linux. You can easily install Git on Linux via the package management tool that usually should come with your distribution.

Debian/Ubuntu

- Here, the git packages are available using the command apt.

- Do make sure that you are only using the latest version of the software. To do so, you shall have to navigate to the command prompt shell and follow it up by running the command sudo apt-get update to ensure that everything is up-to-date.

- For installing Git, run the command sudo apt-get install git-all.

- Once your command output has been completed, you should be able to verify your installation by using the command: git version.

Fedora

- Git packages can be used using the command dnf.

- In order to be able to install Git, navigate to the command prompt shell followed by using the command: sudo dnf install git-all.

- Once your command output has been completed, you should be able to verify the installation by using your command: git version.

Some Elementary Functions

Depending on your operating system, many of you, as mentioned in the previous section, will have Git pre-installed in your PCs. But getting started certainly means more than only having the software installed into your system. To start, it is imperative that you know as well as are well-versed with the basics of how Git tends to work. The actual work itself can be done in a terminal, an app like say, a GitHub Desktop, or even through GitHub.com. But keep in mind that a terminal window tends to be the best option because it will give you access to all of Git's functionalities, whereas if you interact with Git through GitHub, your experience is bound to be limited since local tools of this kind can only give you the most popular Git functionalities to work your way around in the software, i.e., not all of them.

There are several ways that you could make use of to operate within Git, but this does not necessarily make our work easier. On the contrary, one of the most talked-about demerits of Git as a software is recognized to be its lack of user-friendliness, a large number of commands that one must have to master, as well as the relatively long time it takes for a developer to consolidate her/his mastery in the subject. So, now, let's learn about the basic functions to that you will have to make use of in a fundamental Git workflow:

Creating Branches

The central branch is known as the master branch. We will need another branch to do our work, so we will fork it out for us and then use a pull request in order to be able to make our changes in a safe manner. So first off, create a working branch from the master. You are allowed to name it whatever you feel like, but it is generally recommended that your branches are named after the central function or feature they purportedly are to focus on. One person could also end up working on numerous branches. Similarly, numerous people might have collaborated for the sake of the feature of a single branch. Meaning that one branch is meant for one purpose and not necessarily one individual. Wherever you are currently working, i.e., wherever your HEAD is pointing toward, or whatever branch you have currently been working and "checked out" on is to be the parent of the branch you shall create. You are allowed to create branches from tags, commits, as well as other branches. But the most common workflow that you will observe as well as perform as part of your work will involve the creation of a feature branch from the main code line, also known as the master, which also happens to represent the most recent production code.

Making Changes and Making Commits

Once you are done with creating your branch and have also made sure to move the HEAD pointer toward it by checking out to that branch, you now are ready to get to the coding part of your work. Using tools like a text editor as well as an Integrated Development Environment (IDE) should help you in making all the necessary changes in your repository. Then, save your changes and you're ready to commit. To initiate your commit, you will have to make use of the command "git add [file]" so that Git knows what changes you wish to be included as well as incorporated. First, save as well as stage your changes, and then you should be prepared to make your commit using the command "git commit -m" "descriptive commit message."

Pushing Your Changes to the Remote

Once you have made a commit, and done so locally, you still remain the only person who has seen it and is aware of its existence. If you want to collaborate and let other people see and review your work, you would have to use the command "git push." If it happens to be your first use of the command, Git will automatically expect more information from you. The command "git push -u origin [branch-name]" will ask Git to push the current branch, as well as create a branch on the remote repository that is a clone of it, with the exact same name, apart from creating a relationship with the same branch, to make sure that this much information will prove sufficient the next time we come around to using

Git push. The command git push, by default, is only capable of pushing the branch that you happen to be currently checked out to. At times, you might find yourself simply be blocked from pushing. This tends to happen because there might be a new commit on a branch in the remote repository. In case of this issue, you need to start out with the command git pull so that you can incorporate the changes from the remote into your own feature branch, as well as resolve any merge conflicts and then complete the merge from the remote to the local branch, followed by trying the push again; this time hopefully successfully so.

Opening a Pull Request

Pushing a branch as well as the new commits to a remote repository is perfectly adequate if a pull request made by you is already in existence. But if it happens to be the first time you are pushing that particular branch, it is imperative that you open a new pull request. A pull request can be primarily understood as a comparison of two disparate branches, they are the master branch, as well as the feature branch, that is usually created from the former. The branches as well as the pull requests therefore tend to be scoped around a particular function or additional work, rather than the person who happens to be making those changes or the amount of time that will be required in order for those changes to be made. Pull requests also allow peers to give you detailed reviews on the codes that you have been working on, letting you know if there are issues that need further looking into or if the changes are good to go.

You must also ensure that your pull requests contain the correct as well as the suitable amount of information.

If your code is undergoing review, there should be no ambiguity around the kind of change that seems to have occurred. You must include information on what a particular change is supposed to be related to, what prompted your decision to make it, what has already been done, what is yet to be done, any specific query that you might have with regard to the help you need or a specific aspect that you seek review on, etc. You could also include links to any related or relevant discussion or work to be able to further enhance the iteration process. Using request templates for situations like these can prove to be of tremendous help. Request templates make the whole process significantly easier by being able to automate the content at the beginning of the body of your pull requests.

Collaborating

This part includes a variety of functions, like getting your reviews as well as feedback, making commits, then pushing them up all over again to get more feedback/insight. Pulling requests tend to be misunderstood as an effective end point to your work, i.e., one is supposed to make use of pull requests when their work is finished. On the contrary, a pull request should be seen as the beginning of your work or at least a beginning of the collaborative aspects of it. The sooner you will open a pull request, the more visibility your team of developers will have to the work that you are doing. Later, when you are prepared to receive feedback, you should be able to acquire it by integrating a variety of tests as well as requesting for reviews from your team members. It is highly likely that you would want to make more changes in your work later on. To make sure that you are able to do that, make several commits on the same branch. Once the new commits have been made available on the remote repository, the pull request should be able to update as well as show you the most up-to-date version of your work.

Merging into Master

Once you as well as your team has reached the conclusion that a particular pull request looks good enough, you should be able to merge it. Merging is the process through which you should be able to integrate a feature branch into most usually, the master branch. When you will be able to do this, your master branch will get updated with changes, and your pull request, subsequently, shall be closed. Do remember to delete your branch after the process of merging has been completed since that branch is superfluous and will not be needed anymore. As mentioned earlier, the branches are usually lightweight as well as cheap, so you should create a fresh one if you feel the need to do so. Additionally, if you do not wish to immediately merge your pull request, you always have the option of closing the pull requests that contain unmerged changes.

The Commands

To learn as well as master all the crucial Git commands, you can always go through the following list:

- **git status:** A very useful command since it should be able to show you which branch you're on, what files are currently present in the working or the staging directory, and any other sort of important information that the software feels you must be made aware of.

- **git clone [url]:** It will help you in creating a clone or downloading a repository that already exists on a hosting platform like GitHub, including all of its branches, files, and commits.

- **git checkout [branch-name]:** This command will switch from your current branch to a specific branch, along with updating the working directory of the software.

- **git branch:** This command is utilized to see the current branches of your local repository. Additionally, you should also be able to use the command "git branch [branch-name]" to create a new branch from the location you are currently in, or the command git branch – all to be able to see all the branches, the local ones as well as the remote tracking ones stored from the last time you used the commands git pull or git fetch from your remote.

- **git commit -m "descriptive message":** This command will record all the file snapshots in your version history permanently.

- **git add [file]:** This command will snapshot the file to prepare it for the process of versioning, by sending it to the staging area.

- **git push:** This command will upload all the commits you have made on your local branch to the remote repository.

- **git pull:** The command git pull is understood as a combination of commands git fetch as well as git merge.

The role of this command is to update the present local working branch with all the new commits that have been made from a corresponding remote branch on a hosting service like GitHub.

- **git remote -v:** This command should be able to show you all the remote repositories that happen to be associated with each other, along with the names with which they have been stored, such as "origin."

- **git log:** This command allows you to browse as well as inspect the evolution of all your project files.

WHAT IS VERSION CONTROL

A VCS is a type of a system that will allow you to keep track of the various changes that were made to a particular code over a specific span of time. Using version control has its own set of advantages. A VCS software should be able to keep track of all the changes that are being made to a code in a special and specific database. This means that at any given point of time, you should be able to go back to the older versions of the code that you were working on. Subsequently, it becomes easier to track the mistakes that were committed as well as rectify them while also ensuring minimum disruption for your team members. Collaborating on a single code therefore becomes significantly more manageable.

A VCS typically involves two elements, a repository and a working copy. The repository can be understood as a database of all the changes that have been made. It contains the edits as well as the historical versions, i.e., the snapshots of the projects. A working copy, variably referred to as a checkout, happens to be the personal copy of all the files that are a part of a particular project. You should be able to edit this copy without affecting the work being done by the other developers as well as commit your changes to the repository when you are done working on them.

Since coding happens to be a fundamental part of the data sciences, it is absolutely essential for you to make use of the version control software to be able to ensure a proper maintenance of the databases along with the source code. All the changes that you are making are being recorded, and a well-conducted streamlining of the group projects will significantly enhance your efficiency. In the absence of a VCS, you and a fellow team member are working on a shared folder as well as the same bunch of files. At some point of time, one individual will inevitably overwrite on the changes made by another. With Version Control Software at your disposal, everybody is allowed to work freely, on any kind of file at any given point of time. The software will later collate all the changes made in a common version. This way, there shall never be any confusion regarding where the latest version of a particular file is; it is always inside your VCS.

Git is one of the most popular VCSs in use today. To be more specific, Git is a DVCS, i.e., it provides peer-to-peer version control, unlike centralized systems, e.g., Subversion. Git will not be storing the changes made in one central repository. This could be an incredibly complicated process since every individual, who happens to be working on a particular project, has to have access to the central repository as well as be able to download the latest version of a particular project to make changes to it. Git will give everyone a localized repository with its own history. So, it becomes this simple as well as efficient tool that can facilitate version control by collaborating with affiliated services like GitHub, which is a Git repository hosting service that also happens to provide task management as well as access control tools for your projects.

Version control is also variously referred to as source control. It has become a very important aspect of high-performing development because alongside the acceleration of the development environments, VCSs are able to help teams work smarter as well as at a much higher speed. It also ensures an increase in successful deployments along with a reduction in the development time, which makes them particularly useful for the DevOps teams, who are supposed to be responsible for combining Information Technology operations with software development.

A source code is critically important for any and every software project. It is a valuable asset that contains the knowledge about the issue at hand that the developers have collated through tremendous effort. A VCS should be able to protect the main code from a potential catastrophe along with the vagaries of human error. Software developers who are working in teams are almost always in the process of writing the source code alongside making changes to the already developed source code. The code for any project or app software is typically arranged as a folder, which is sometimes also referred to as a "file tree." One developer is writing a new source code, and another is fixing a bug by making modifications to that source code only. A good VCS would be able to ensure that the concurrent work being conducted does not clash with each other. Changes that will be made in one part of the software, at some point of time, are bound to be incompatible with the work that is being done by a different coder in another part of the system. These issues are not only to be discovered but also resolved without creating any obstructions for the development that is being made by the remainder of the team. Furthermore, any change that will be made to the code could lead to the development of more bugs. So, a code has to be continuously tested, and a good VCS will make sure that the development as well the testing proceed smoothly until a new code is created as well as completed.

Additionally, a good VCS should ideally be able to work on any platform rather than offering the prescription of an Operating System that a coder must necessarily use. It is imperative that we support a coder's preferred workflow rather than imposing upon her/him a particular methodology of work. In the absence of a VCS, the software development team is sure to run into problems like the incorporation of incompatible changes that have to subsequently be separated, figured out, and reworked, which can be a painstaking as well as a strenuous process. Looking at it this way, the powerful advantages embedded within the features of VCSs are magnified even more as the software development teams scale up and include even more coders, wherein the VCSs will be playing an indispensable role for the sake of the preservation of the speed, efficiency, and the agility of the development teams.

VCSs can be classified into two different types: Source Code Management (SCM) and Revision Control Systems (RCS).

RCSs work effectively as standalone applications. So, the applications like spreadsheets and word processors are embedded with various mechanisms that control the various versions of the files being worked upon. The SCM tools, on the other hand, are utilized for coding applications, their prominent examples being Git, Subversion, etc. VCSs could also have a significant number of unique features, for example, the user is provided with an up-to-date history for a variety of files, there is no requirement for a different kind of a repository system, the repositories also allow themselves to be cloned as per the needs as well as the availability of the members of the coding team. This last feature, specifically, can prove to be a life-saver if there happen to be cases of accidental deletions as well as system failures. Furthermore, VCS tends to come along with a tag system that can help the users to be able to differentiate between alpha, beta, and several other release versions for a multitude of documents. Irrespective of the kind of VCS that one seems to be working with, they tend to offer you the necessary facility of being traceable. Every alteration made cannot just be tracked but, significantly, also annotated to highlight the purpose and the reasoning of the coder, as well as its connection with the larger project that is being developed. This should allow the coders to be able to make appropriate changes which are in accordance with the long-term design that has been prepared keeping a particular system in mind. This really helps if you happen to be working on the legacy codes because it helps the developers to assess the quantity of future work that might be required with a fairly decent degree of accuracy.

There is also another way that can be utilized if you wish to divide the VCSs into three types:

- **Local VCS:** A local VCS will keep track of your files within the local system. This approach is used pretty commonly and is also quite simple, but prone to errors, because the odds of you writing into the wrong file are much higher. RCS happens to be one of the most common VCS tools. It keeps a set of patches, i.e., the difference between the files in a special format on disk. When you add up the patches, the VCS is able to recreate what any file might have looked like at that particular point of time.

- **Centralized VCS:** In this case, the centralized server is able to record all the changes that have been made into the file. The server also contains information about the several versions of the main files as well as a list of clients who happen to have access to the same files. TortoiseSVN, a Subversion client that has been implemented as a Microsoft Windows shell extension, in order to be able to help the programmers in the management of the different versions of source code that is the basis of their programs, can be cited as a good example of a centralized VCS.

  - In the case of centralized VCSs, two actions are incredibly important to make sure that your changes are visible to others: that you commit and that they update.

  - The benefits of using centralized VCSs are the following. They will make the collaboration between the developers fairly easy while also providing insight on what everyone else happens to be doing vis-à-vis a particular project. Further, it also allows the administrators a fine-grained sense of control over who is able to do what.

- There are some demerits as well that propelled the development of DVS. The most obvious among them is a potential point of failure which the centralized repository might become if it happens to go down at a point when the collaboration as well as the saving of the versioned changes has not been possible. Or the hard disk of the central database could become corrupted while no backups are present as well. You could possibly lose everything.

- **DVCS/DVS:** Distributed VCS was developed so that it could overcome the limitations of the centralized VCS. The clients can completely replicate the repository and its full history. If a server happens to die, the client repositories have to be copied to the server so that it is able to be revived. Each clone has a full backup of all the data. Git, the focus of the previous section, is a good, immensely popular, as well as successful, example of a distributed VCS (DVCS). Mercurial is another. These VCSs play an incredibly important part in helping the developers overcome the problems caused by a single point of failure.

  - A DVCS also contains multiple repositories. Every user tends to have their own repository as well as a working copy. Merely committing your changes will not be able to give others the access to the said changes. This tends to be so because a commit will end up reflecting the changes of the file present in your local repository, and you shall have to push them so that they are visible on the central repository as well. Likewise, whenever you make an update, you will not be able to acquire the changes others have made unless you first pull them into your own repository. So there is a four-step process involved in the workflow: you commit, and then you push, they pull, and then, they update.

While it is absolutely possible to be able to work on projects without VCS, this software has become so omnipresent that doing so would involve an incredible risk that you wouldn't find many software development teams willing to partake in. The moot question that remains is not whether we should use a VCS, but what kind of VCS might prove to be the most suitable for our needs. Some of the examples of the VCSs that are available for various software development teams are Mercurial, Git, SVN (i.e., Subversion), Concurrent Version System (CVS), etc. Mercurial happens to be a freely available Source Control Management (SCM) tool which is adept at handling projects with a variety of complexity, due to its intuitive as well as easy to handle interface. While CVS utilizes the distributed application structure in order to be able to conduct software development, SVN is a CollabNet-created free VCS which should be able to store as well as manage your TestComplete test projects along with your project suites.

You could also keep these handy tips and tricks in mind that can be used for the smooth functioning of a variety of VCSs, whether it be the centralized or the distributed VCS:

- Write good as well as descriptive commit messages. This can be incredibly useful for somebody who happens to be examining a change and therefore must understand the purpose as well as the intent behind a change, if you are able to convey the same with good clarity. If the reviewer is examining changes related to a particular concept, it is very likely that they will look through your commit messages. Commits happen to be elementary units that you require in order to be able to work on Git. In the absence of commits, you will not be able to share your work with other developers.

- You must make sure that every commit has only one purpose and that it focuses on implementing the same. The central aim of version history is rendered completely redundant if your commit contains codes for multiple different reasons or if the changes made in a code for a particular purpose are spread across many different commits.

- Absolutely avoid making commits indiscriminately and make sure that you are using selected, as well as specific files, in order to be able to record your commits. Limit your commits and ensure that you never commit more than you intended to.

- You will have to incorporate the modifications that have been made by the other team members as well as ensure that you happen to be working on the most updated version of the main file. If you are able to do so, you will be avoiding potential conflicts as well as incompatibilities that are sure to come if the two commands happen to go against each other.

- Parallelly to the last point made, you shall have to make sure that you share your changes with your colleagues and fellow developers as soon as you possibly can, i.e., before you go on to make other changes to your file. This is to say that you must establish a coordination routine along with your team members to ensure that there are minimum situations pertaining to conflicts. In order for you to achieve these purposes, Git gives you the option to create a Bare Git repository. A repository can be usually created by using the git init command apart from the git init –bare command. The repositories that are created by making use of the former command, in the Git's jargon, are known as working directories, while those repos that were created by making use of the latter command are called bare repos. Working Directories and Bare Repos are structurally distinct. While the former is used for purposes related to work, the latter is only meant to be shared with fellow coders in a centralized place where everybody is able to record their changes. Since Git happens to be a distributed VCS, no one has the permission to or will be able to directly modify the file that is present in the shared centralized repository. So, the coders have no choice but to clone the bare repo that is shared with everyone working on a particular project and then make the required changes within their respective working copies. Subsequently, these changes have to be made available to their other team members. Because a bare repo will never be edited, it shall not be having a working tree.

- Make sure that you do not use overlong lines, keeping the limit of each sentence to a maximum of 80 characters. If you use long lines, there is a good chance that several edits will come within the same line and later conflict with each other. Additionally, make sure that you do not reedit, refill, or rejustify the paragraphs. It will end up changing every single line of the paragraph, making it highly difficult to determine what sorts of changes were made as part of every commit.

- Make sure that you are not committing generated files to version control. VCS is supposed to be there for the files that have to be edited. For example, you need not commit .pdf files because they have been generated from a text formatting application. But you should be able to commit the source files that have been used for the generation of the same .pdf files.

- Be familiar with the merge tools. It is highly likely that you shall end up creating conflicts if you are stressed out about meeting a forthcoming deadline, are going through a bad mental health day, etc. Being well-versed with your merge tool will help you cope better, given your circumstances.

- Lastly, never forget that you have to obtain as well as store your own copy of the project file, which is also known as "checking out" as well as "cloning."

To reiterate, VCS is very useful because it helps you keep track of changes that you made within a script. It gives you the agency to choose when you believe you have reached a stage in your code which seems to be worth saving as well as keeping track of, functions like data analysis, enabling collaboration, tracking who changed what, etc. VCSs tend to render a plethora of advantages to coders as well as developers:

- It will be able to enhance your project development speed by providing as well as improving upon the possibilities of efficient collaboration.

- A VCS will leverage your productivity, expedite the product delivery, and the skills of your employees via better communication as well as assistance.

- Reduction in the possibility of errors as well as conflicts, while making the project development traceable to small changes.

- The contributors or the employees should be able to contribute from anywhere, irrespective of their geographical locations.

- Ease of recovery in case of a disaster or a contingent situation.

- It will inform us about the Who, What, When, Why, of all the changes that have been made.

WHAT IS GITHUB?

Now, we move on to GitHub. If you happen to be wondering where Git ends and where the affiliated services like GitHub tend to begin, you are in company. This is because Git and

GitHub are tied closely together, which makes working on them a tremendously seamless experience. While Git is supposed to take care of the underlying version control, GitHub is the platform providing many opportunities for collaboration that is built on top of Git. GitHub is the place where you will be pulling requests, reviews, comments, integrated tests, and a lot more. Most developers stick to Git for their local coding work and then utilize GitHub for the purposes of collaborative work. The collaborative work can range from the utilization of GitHub to host the shared remote repositories, to the work with colleagues as well as the capitalization on features such as code reviews, protected branches, GitHub actions, and several others. If you are already well-versed with Git, and have to sign up for a GitHub account, you shall have to head over to github.com.

The company GitHub, Inc. is an Internet hosting provider for the purposes of version control as well as software development while one is making use of Git. The company offers services like distributed version control as well as SCM functionality that is also provided by Git, apart from several other features that are original to it. GitHub will give you collaboration features like bug tracking, task management, feature requests, continuous integration, wikis, and the access control for various projects that you shall choose to undertake. With its head offices in California, GitHub has been a subsidiary of Microsoft ever since the multinational technology conglomerate acquired it in 2018. Generally, GitHub is utilized to host several open-source projects. GitHub is supposed to have more than 190 million repositories, with as many as 28 million public repositories which are included in that number. As of November 2021, GitHub currently has over 73 million users, and is the world's largest code hosting service. A large percentage of the existing Git repositories are hosted by GitHub, and various open-source projects make use of the provider for purposes of Git Hosting, issue tracking, code review, and others. So yes, GitHub might not be a direct part of the Git project, but there is a high chance that you will want to or shall have to interact with GitHub at some point, if you are to continue to operate on Git professionally.

Now, let's look into how we should be able to use GitHub professionally as well as effectively. First and foremost, we would learn how to set up as well as configure our account. The first thing you would have to do is set up a free user account. For this, you would have to visit github.com, choose a suitable username that is yet to be taken, and provide your email address and the password, following it up by clicking on the green "Sign Up for GitHub" button.

After you pass through the GitHub sign up form, the next thing you need to do is to go through the pricing page to check out the upgraded plans. However, as a learner and a beginner, you do not have to do anything on this page for now. GitHub should also be sending you an email so that it can verify the email address that you provided. It is imperative that you avoid skipping this step and complete the entire verification process. Following this, you should be able to see the OctoCat logo near the top-left your screen. Clicking on it should take you to the dashboard page of your account. Now, you are all set to make use of GitHub for your coding projects.

Important to note, GitHub provides nearly all of its functions in the free accounts, barring a few advanced features. GitHub's paid services will give you advanced tools and features, along with higher limits for the free services that are already available. GitHub will offer you three plans: Free, Team, and Enterprise. The Free Plan will render you the basic services for individuals and the organizations as well. These include the following:

- Community support.

- 500 MB worth of package storage (for the public repositories).

- New projects as well as issues, albeit with a limited beta.

- 2000 automation minutes per month (for the public repositories).

- Limitless private as well as public repositories.

The team package is supposed to be used for advanced collaboration between individuals and organizations. This package provides everything that is available in the free pack, as well as:

- Web-based support.

- 2 GB Package Storage.

- Pages as well as Wikis.

- 3000 automation minutes per month (free for public repositories).

- Codeowners.

- Required reviewers for pull requests.

- Ability to draft pull requests.

- Protected branches.

The Enterprise package will give you compliance security as well as a flexible deployment. Its features include everything that will be provided by the Team (and Free) package apart from other benefits like:

- 50,000 automation minutes per month (free for public repositories).

- 50 GB of packages storage (free for public repositories).

- GitHub connect.

- Security Assertion Markup Language (SAML) single sign on. This feature is generally used for the purposes of online security. SAML will allow you to access a number of web applications by making use of a single set of login credentials.

- Advanced auditing.
- Automatic version updates as well as security.

You would also be provided with such other exclusive add-ons as:

- Token, Secret, and Code Scanning.
- Premium Support.

The free package, needless to say, is free of cost. On the other hand, the Team as well as the Enterprise packages should cost you $4 and $21 per user per month, respectively.

SSH Access

Now, it is easy for you to connect with the Git repositories by using the https://protocol. You must authenticate with your username as well as password that you must have used during the setup process itself. However, if you just have to clone public projects, you do not even need to sign up. Your account will come into play when you wish to fork your projects or use the push command. If you wish to learn how to use the Secure Shell Remotes (SSH), you will first have to configure a public key. If you don't have one, you must get it generated. The process for this is similar across all the operating systems. But first, you will have to check that you already do not have one. Generally, by default, the SSH keys of a user are stored within that particular user's ~/.ssh directory. You will also be able to see if you already have a key by being able to go to that directory and listing its contents. If you did not find your private key, or an unassociated public key, and if you also don't have a

.ssh directory, you need to be able to create them by using a program called ssh-keygen which is provided by the SSH package on the MacOS as well as the Linux systems and alongside Git for the Windows.

First, open your account settings by pressing on the settings icon available at the top right of your window. Then, click on the "SSH Keys" section on the left-hand side of your screen. Press on the button "Add an SSH key" and follow it up by giving a name to your key, pasting the contents of the public key into the provided text area, and lastly clicking on the button "Add Key." You must be careful to remember naming your SSH key something that you should be able to remember later on. Use clear names for keys like "Work Laptop," "Work Account," etc. This should prove to be useful because it will allow you to revoke a key later on since you will be easily able to tell what you are looking for.

Your Avatar

Next, if you want to do it, you can replace the avatar that will be generated with an image of your choosing. First, click on the tab "Profile" (located above the SSH keys tab) and then press on "Upload new picture." Crop your image as you deem fit, then click on the button "Set new profile picture." Now, wherever you will interact with people on the site, they should be able to see your avatar and your username as well. If you had uploaded an avatar earlier to the immensely popular Gravatar service (mostly used for WordPress accounts), that avatar will be in use by default, and you would not have to perform this step at all.

Email Addresses

Your email address is particularly important on GitHub. This is so because GitHub will map your Git commits to your user via the use of your email ID. If you tend to use multiple email addresses while completing your commits and you need to ensure that GitHub will link them up properly, you can add all the email addresses you have used so far as well as those that you intend to use in the future to the Emails tab that you will be able to find in the Admin section. Now, for the "Add Email Addresses" section, you will be able to see some of the states that you can possibly use. The address at the top is generally the one that is verified and gets set as your primary address. This means that if GitHub wants to send you the notifications as well as the receipts, they will get sent at this address. The second address should also be verified, and so you are allowed to set it as your primary if you wish to do so. Further, if you have also decided to make use of an unverified email address, that is perfectly okay, but keep in mind that GitHub will not be allowing you to turn it into your primary email address, even if you want to do so. If GitHub will see any of the provided email addresses in your commit messages section in any repository available on the site, it will automatically link it to you/your user from now on.

Two-Factor Authentication

Finally, for supplementary security, you will need to set up your Two-Factor Authentication, also called "2FA." 2FA is a type of an authentication mechanism that is becoming more and more popular these days to mitigate the risk of your GitHub account getting compromised if your password is stolen. You shall have to turn it on, and GitHub will then ask you to conduct two different methods of authentication, so that if one of them happens to get compromised, the attacker still shall not be able to access your account.

You would be able to find the 2FA set-up under the "Security" Tab in your account settings. First, you must click on the "Set up two-factor authentication" button. This would take you to a configuration page wherein you will have to choose to make use of a phone app so that you could generate your secondary code, which will be a "time-based one-time password," or alternatively, you could ask GitHub to reach out to you via a code that the company should SMS you every time you have to log in.

Now that you have made a choice on what method you shall prefer as well as followed the mentioned instructions to set up your 2FA, your account will definitely be significantly more secure, and you shall also have to provide a code as well as a password if you feel the need to login to GitHub, to ensure that your account is never jeopardized because of issues pertaining to security.

History of GitHub

The development of the GitHub.com platform was initiated on October 19, 2007. The official website was launched in April 2008 by Chris Wanstrath, Tom Preseten-Werner, P.J. Hyett, as well as Scott Chacon after it had already been available for some months as a beta release. GitHub, Inc. was originally supposed to be a flat organization, with no middle managers at all. The company had also ensured the adoption of the principle of self-management, so that every worker was encouraged to play a manager for her/himself. Not just that, GitHub's employees could choose to work on projects that they were interested in (open allocation), and amenable to work for, even though the salaries were to be determined by the chief executive officer. In 2014 later on, the organization had to introduce a set of middle-management officers in order to be able to ensure better efficiency in handling its affairs.

GitHub actually started out as a bootstrapped start-up business, which in its early years had to be managed so that it could generate sufficient revenue for it to be funded solely by its three co-founders, who were then able to take on employees. Four years after the company was officially launched, Andreessen Horowitz invested a hundred million dollars in venture capital in it. July 2015 witnessed GitHub raising another $250 million worth of venture capital in round B series. This time, the investors were Sequoia Capital, Andreessen Horowitz, and Thrive Capital, along with other venture capital funds. By the time July 2021 came around, GitHub had made a cumulative of $650 million, as per the Annual Recurring Revenue. GitHub was also developed by Chris Wanstrath, P.J. Hyett, Tom Preseten-Werner, and Scott Chacon, a server-side web application framework that was written in the programming language Ruby under MIT's License. While the company's primary service began in February 2008, the company itself had existed since 2007, its main office present in San Francisco, California. On February 24, 2009, just in its second year yet, the company declared that within the first year of having been online, it had managed to accumulate more than 46,000 public repositories, 17,000 out of which were created in the last month, i.e., January 2009 itself. At that point of time, about 6200 repositories had been forked at least once, while 4600 had been merged. In the same year, the official page of GitHub had been harnessed by more than 100,000 users and had also grown to host 90,000 separate public repositories, 12,000 of which had been forked at least one time, to make up a grand total of 135,000 repositories. By 2010, GitHub was hosting more than a million repositories. A year more passed, and this number had doubled. ReadWriteWeb, a web technology blog, had reported that GitHub was successful in surpassing other SCM companies like SourceForge, GoogleCode, etc., as far as the sum total of commits made from the time span of January to May 2011 were concerned. Then, on the date of January 16, 2013, GitHub officially passed the mark of 3 million users and was subsequently hosting over 5 million repositories. By the end of the year came, the number of total repositories had doubled again, the number now at 10 million. In 2012, GitHub demonstrated its ability to raise $100 million worth of funds from Andreessen Horowitz with a valuation of $750 million. On July 29, 2015, it was again reported how GitHub had raised funds worth $250 million in a round led by Sequoia Capital, an American company focusing on venture capital firm. There were other investors in that round as well like Andreessen Horowitz, Institutional Venture Partners (IVP), and Thrive Capital, known for investing in technology companies for the most part. This round valued the company at around $2 billion. In 2015, it was witnessed GitHub opening its first office outside of the United States, in Tokyo, the capital of Japan. Then, in 2016, the company ended up making an appearance in the

Forbes Cloud 100 list at the rank of 14. However, this honor has eluded it since. On February 28, 2018, the company fell victim to the third biggest distributed denial-of-service attack (DDoS) in history, with the incoming traffic peaking at around 1.35 terabytes per second. On June 19, 2018, GitHub expanded to GitHub Education and began offering free education bundles to schools.

Acquired by Microsoft

In 2012, Microsoft became an important customer as well as a significant user of the GitHub, utilizing services provided to allow itself to host open-source projects and development tools like Chakra Core, .NET Core, PowerShell, MS Build, Visual Studio Code, Power Toys, Windows Terminal, Windows Calculator, and a bulk of its product documentation (now available on Microsoft Docs). Then, on June 4, 2018, the company went a step further and expressed its intent to acquire GitHub for the price of $7.5 billion. This deal was closed on October 26, 2018. GitHub, however, still continues its operations independently as a platform, community, and a business. Under the tutelage of Microsoft, the service had to come under the leadership of Xamarin's Nat Friedman, who reported to the Executive Vice-President of Microsoft Cloud & AI, Scott Guthrie. The GitHub CEO Chris Wanstrath was retained as a "technical fellow," with him reporting to Guthrie too. However, this acquisition was accompanied with its lot of controversies. Developers like Kyle Simpson, author and JavaScript trainer, and Rafael Laguna, CEO, Open-Xchange (a web-oriented communication, collaboration, and office productivity software suite) expressed their uneasiness and concerns regarding

Microsoft's purchase, citing the company's handling, or mishandling, as they understood it, of previous purchases, like Skype, Nokia's mobile business, etc.

This acquisition was in line with the business strategy of the corporation under the CEO Satya Nadella, which laid a tremendous emphasis on the cloud computing services, and their contributions to the development of opensource software. In 2016, Microsoft was at the top of a list of ten multiple organizations with the most open-source contributors to GitHub. Harvard Business Review, however, asserted that Microsoft's intention to acquire GitHub was simply and only to get access to its user base, which it should be able to use as a loss leader, to encourage the use of its other development products as well as services. The concerns that were expressed over GitHub's sale ended up benefitting its competitors, at least for some time. GitLab, a commercial open-source software that provides a hosted service VCS, Bitbucket, owned by Atlassian, and SourceForge, owned by BizX, reported that they had recipient bolstered interest from the market, with spikes in their new users who wanted to migrate their projects from GitHub to their respective services. GitHub then acquired Semmle, a code analysis tool in September 2019. February 2020 would see GitHub being launched in India with much fanfare under a new name, GitHub India Private Limited. Later, GitHub acquired npm, a vendor for JavaScript packaging, priced at an undisclosed amount of money, thus closing the deal on April 15, 2020. In July 2020, the GitHub Archive Program went on to be founded, so that GitHub could archive its open-source code for future.

Mascot

GitHub's mascot is called an "octocat," an anthropomorphized organism with five octopus-like arms. This character was a brainchild of the graphic designer Simon Oxley as a clipart that he was initially supposed to sell on iStock, a provider of online royalty-free, international microstock photography based in Canada. GitHub became interested in Oxley's work after Twitter chose a bird designed by him as their logo. The illustration that GitHub eventually zeroed in on was a character that Oxley called "Octopuss." Because GitHub wanted Octopuss as their logo (a use which the iStock license could not permit), they ended up negotiating with Oxley so that they could buy the exclusive rights of the created image. GitHub rechristened Octopuss to Octocat and then trademarked the character itself along with the new name. Later on, GitHub also hired an illustrator called Cameron McEfee so that they could adapt Octocat for multiple different purposes on their website as well as for the promotional materials; McEfee and several other GitHub users have, since then created, many hundreds of variations of this character, which can be found on the GitHub Octodex.

So, even though there were several prospective preachers who should have spread the open-source religion, whether it was the Google Code or the SourceForge, GitHub eventually defeated them all. When Git released in 2005, open-source was already going through something of a renaissance. Interest and desire to adopt Linux, for example, was immensely strong. The first Web 2.0 applications had also emerged. Many companies were now preferring to migrate their tech stacks to the open-source servers that were then available. Although Git had made collaboration on the open-source projects efficient and effortless by introducing the practice of forking, there was still a thing that Git could not possibly do: help the coders in their search for the mentioned open-source projects. A lot of programmers had been working on many exciting open-source projects, but finding them in itself remained a remarkably difficult task.

It is this chasm that GitHub wanted to fill, and managed to do so in time as well, passing with flying colors. When Hyett and Wanstrath started working on what eventually became GitHub in 2007, both of them had been working as programmers for a technology website known as CNET (the full form being Computer Network). Both of them had liked the development framework that was being offered by Ruby on Rails. While also holding their day jobs, Hyett and Wanstrath developed multiple suggestions as well as improvements for the codebase of their favorite Rails. However, at that point of time, no one was really interested in looking at their code. As was the standard procedure for most open-source projects of the time, Rails' codebase was constantly checked by a small and tight-knit group of coders who would manage the contributions that were being made to the main code manually. They were supposed to be the project gatekeepers, and even if, say one of them had ended up liking the work done by Wanstrath and Hyett, the merging of patches for real was not a simple process in any way whatsoever.

On some level, making contributions to Rails had become a matter of who you knew, rather than what you knew. It is so serendipitous then that their enduring contribution would be GitHub, an essential provider tool and hosting service for Git today, because Torvalds' conception as well as understanding of Git, too, was in many ways rooted in ideas like democratization of code development, allowing the developers leeway to collaborate on projects with minimal gatekeeping. Anyhow, despite the significant convenience that Git provided to the developers, there was also this problem of an incredible lack of collaborative tools for it. Sharing code between two developers in itself was an arduous process, taking up a significant amount of time as well as resources. Software developers would have to email patches between themselves until the changes in the code would be able to resolve whatever issue was cropping up. So, it becomes easy to see why something like GitHub was so badly needed. Other developments were also on offer for the improvement of Git. The software was used to primarily rely on the Command Line Interface, but the GUI was developed for it later on as well. Preston-Werner, a Ruby programmer from the Bay area, had begun working on a project known as "Grit," which was conceived of as a tool that would allow the coders to be able to access Git repositories in an object-oriented manner using the language Ruby on Rails. The objective was clear: to develop a place that could host entire code libraries as well as allow programmers to be able to work on code projects in a more collaborative manner, along with learning more about Git as well as its uses. As Preston-Werner imagined it, it would be a "Git hub."

How to Use GitHub

GitHub is a web-based platform that is utilized for version control. Git, on the other hand, works well for simplifying the process of working with the other developers, fostering a spirit as well as the practical possibilities of collaboration. Team members are expected to work on their respective files and later merge the changes made into the master, i.e., the main branch of the project. The skills pertaining to Git as well as GitHub have slowly but surely been promoted from preferred skills to must-have skills for a number of job roles.

How to Create a Repository on GitHub?

A repository is supposed to be a storage space for your product. The repository can be either local, i.e., available on a folder within your system or a useful storage space provided by an online host, like GitHub. You would need to be able to keep your code files, images, text files, or any other types of files in a particular repository. You will also require a GitHub repository for the development of your project, when you have finished making changes to your files, and they are now polished and prepared to be uploaded. The GitHub repository shall therefore be acting as your remote repository. If you wish to create a repository on GitHub, follow the given steps:

- Pay a visit to the site GitHub.com. Fill out the Sign-Up form and then press on the button "Sign up for GitHub."

- Click on the choice "Start a new project."

- Provide a name for your repository, and then follow it up by pressing on the button "Create Repository." You are also expected to provide a description of your repository, though this is completely optional.

Next, you might notice that by default, a GitHub repository is public, meaning that anyone should be able to see the contents of your repository or project. In case of a private repository, that comes alongside the paid version of GitHub, you would be able to choose the entities to whom you want to allow access to your repository as well as what it contains. Additionally, you would be able to initialize your repository via a README file. The README file usually contains the description of your file, and once you check this box, it becomes the first file in your repository. Now, your repository has been successfully created, and you should be ready to make your commits, push, pull, and perform all the important operations. Now, we will move on to understanding branching in GitHub.

Creating Branches

Branches shall be helping you work on multiple versions of a repository at one time. You might also want to add on a new feature (still in the developmental phase) but could be unsure of whether making changes to the central code line would be worth it. Git Branching to the rescue! Branches should allow you to move back and forth between different versions of your project. In the aforementioned scenario, you will be well-advised to fork out a branch and test the new feature without any adverse effects on the main branch. Once your changes are tried, tested, and approved, you should be able to merge your changes from the new branch to the main branch. Here, the main branch refers to the master branch that is present in your repository by default.

To be able to create a new branch within GitHub, you shall need to follow the provided set of instructions:

- First, click on the drop-down option that says "Branch: master."

- The moment you click on the branch, you shall be able to find an existing branch or you shall have to create one. Let us say we will create a branch and subsequently name it "readme-changes." Post creating the new branch, you shall have two branches in your repository, the readme, i.e., the master branch and the branch readme-changes. The new branch is a mere clone of the master branch. To make it different, you will have to make changes via several operations that we shall now delve into.

Making Commits

Committing should be able to save changes to your file. A commit would ideally be accompanied by a message that justifies as well as explains the changes that have been made. The commit message is not compulsory, yet is strongly recommended by nearly all organizations, for the purposes of differentiation, as well as helping the collaborators understand the history of a file as well as the changes that need to be made. To make your first commit on GitHub, follow the provided steps in a proper chronological order:

- Click on the "readme-changes" file that we had created in the previous section.

- Click on "Edit" or a pencil icon that you should be able to find among the right-most corner of this file.

- Once you manage to click on it, your editor shall open wherein you would be able to type out the changes needed.

- Write a commit message that identifies the changes that have been made (recollect the line-wise format: describe changes-blank-explanation of changes).

- Click on option of "Commit Changes" in the end.

Pull Command

The Pull command would have to be one of the most significant commands in GitHub. It informs you about the changes that have been made to a file, request your fellow contributors to view it, and merge it with the master branch as well. Once a commit has been made, anyone should be able to pull the file and initiate a discussion on the change/s. Once the iteration process is complete, the file/s would be merged. If there happen to be any significant conflicts between the different changesets, they would have to be resolved to complete the merge. Now, let us go through the various steps involved to conduct a pull request on GitHub:

- Click on the "Pull Requests" tab.

- Press on "New Pull Request."

- After clicking on the pull request, select the branch and click on the file to be able to view the changes between the two files that are present in our repository.

- Click on "Create Pull Request."

- Enter the title, description of your changes, followed up by clicking on "Create pull request."

Merge Command

Via the use of the Merge command, we should be able to merge the changes made into the master branch. If you wish to use the Merge command on GitHub, you would have to follow these steps in a chronological fashion:

- Click on the "Merge pull request" to merge your changes into the master branch.

- Press on "Confirm Merge."

- You will be able to delete a branch once all of its changes have been incorporated, and if there were no conflicts.

Cloning as well as Forking GitHub Repository

Cloning is essential because it helps us download the codes from remote repositories as well as make suitable changes to them through the use of commits. If you wish to clone on GitHub, you would need to press the green-colored button that contains the text "Clone or Download."

Forking is performed because you wish to create a new branch and then make changes to the main code line, while mostly focusing on one particular feature, the new branch that is created is usually referred to as a feature branch. A few pointers that you ought to be keep in mind about Forking:

- Changes that are made to the original repository should get reflected back to the forked repository.

- If you make changes in a forked repository, they shall not be reflected to the original repository until and unless you would call for a pull request.

In order to be able to fork a repository in GitHub, ensure that you follow the provided sequence of steps:

- Go to the Explore section and conduct a search on the public repositories.

- You would have to open a repository, and you will be able to find a number besides the "Fork" button that tells you how many times it has been forked previously. Click on the button "fork."

After you click on Fork, it should take some time for the software to be able to give you your own local version of the public repository. Once you are done, you would be able to notice the name of that particular repository under your account. Congratulations! You have now successfully managed to fork out an existing repository under your own account on GitHub.

Different Types of Accounts

On GitHub, your user account is your identity for all important purposes. Your user account is also allowed to be a member of as many organizations as you wish to be affiliated with. Organizations tend to belong the enterprise accounts.

Personal User Accounts

Every person who would use GitHub shall have a personal account, which would include:

- Limitless private as well as public repositories alongside GitHub free

- No set limit on the collaborators needed (GitHub Free)

- Supplementary features for private repositories alongside GitHub Pro

- Allows collaboration for work on repositories

Do remember that you shall be allowed to make use of a single account for several purposes, for personal use as well as business purposes. It is generally recommended that you should avoid creating several accounts since it might ensue problems. However, GitHub would provide you the facility to be able to conduct a merge of several user accounts together. Not only that, while the GitHub user accounts are intended to be used by humans, you could also give one to a robot as well, like a continuous integration bot, if you need to do so.

Organization Accounts

Organization accounts are defined as shared accounts wherein huge groups of people are able to collaborate across multiple projects at the same time. Administrators or the owners manage access of various members to the data of an organization as well as projects through a bunch of administrative features as well as a system of robust, sophisticated security. A number of features that you shall be able to find in organization accounts are the following:

- Unlimited membership with a number of roles that will grant you different levels of access to an organization as well as the associated data.

- An ability to give their members a series of access permissions to the repositories of their organization.

- Nested teams that reflect your group or company's structure with a number of cascading access mentions as well as permissions.

- The ability for the owners of a particular organization to check the 2FA status of its members.

- The option to make the 2FA mandatory for all the members of the project.

You need to be able to make use of organization accounts for free via GitHub Free. The facilities would include unlimited repositories with all features, unlimited collaborators to work on your projects with, and unlimited private repositories with limited features. For supplementary features, like better support coverage, sophisticated user authentication as well as management, you would have to upgrade to GitHub Team or GitHub Enterprise Cloud. If you are using the latter, in particular, you shall have the option to purchase the license for GitHub Advanced Security and make use of the features of private repositories.

Enterprise Accounts
Through enterprise accounts, you should be able to manage billing as well as policy for multiple GitHub.com organizations at the same time. Enterprise accounts are generally available with GitHub Enterprise Cloud as well as GitHub Enterprise Server.

With this, we have come to the end of our chapter on Git and GitHub. In this chapter, we talked about what Git is, as well as a number of aspects of Version Control and GitHub. In the next chapter, we move to the central concern of this book, GitHub Pages, and its basics. Let's move on.

CHAPTER 2

What Are GitHub Pages?

IN THIS CHAPTER

➤ What are GitHub Pages?

➤ Basics of GitHub Pages

The previous chapter had us discussing a set of subjects like Git, Version Control, GitHub, etc. In this chapter, we move GitHub Pages, introducing the subject as well as the basic concepts that are associated with it.

WHAT ARE GITHUB PAGES?

The primary utility of GitHub Pages lies in how it will allow you to effortlessly, and for free, create a website using GitHub. You do not have to be a professional or an expert, and the process is incredibly simple. So, you

DOI: 10.1201/9781003242055-2

need to begin learning about GitHub Pages to have an easy and quick guide that will allow you to create as well as publish a blog, a website, a free portfolio, etc. It is an effective tool that people are not even aware about having access to. With an understanding of GitHub on your fingertips, you should be able to turn any repository on GitHub into a website using the click of a few Burton's. The said website could be an online portfolio of your work for your potential employers to go through or a blog or a business website that you need to create for professional purposes. Or you could simply not have the budget or the desire for dealing with issues like website hosting, domain names, etc.

But you might ask, Why should I even have a website in the first place? A website is an important aspect of your professional discourse. It is hard to imagine someone who shall not be benefitted from having a website of their own. You will have a strong display of your portfolio for your potential employers as well as clients. You could organize your projects in a manner that can be shared with other people. You might also want to create a blog that talks about the things you have done, the places you have to, the experiences you have had, etc. Or you might simply have a utilitarian need to advertise your business or yourself or just sell a product or a service that you are offering. You could have multiple other specific reasons of your own, but, basically and ultimately, you wish to put a thing together without spending a tremendous amount of time, money, or resources on it.

A website is crucial because it is a method of connecting with the people of the world as well as an incredibly powerful tool for communication. A website is how you share your work, your passions, and your interests. It allows you to build, develop, and curate your online image. Furthermore, the faster you will develop your site, the more time you shall have to be able to not only just build your online presence but also reach out to potential customers as well as other people that you really seek to reach. A good website is a strong tool in your arsenal that might help you stand out from a sea of competitors. Nevertheless, it isn't an easy thing to do if you lack the technical know-how and are starting from scratch. A couple of popular ways that a beginner should be able to utilize to create a free as well as a simple website are GitHub and WordPress. WordPress can be of tremendous help to the beginners who need all the help that they can get. A typical feature of a WordPress website is that it is obvious to any viewer that they are on a WordPress site. This would be easy to establish because you will have a URL ending with word-press.com as well as a WordPress logo at the bottom of every page. As far as GitHub is concerned, you will find that if you are starting out in the world of technology, you will look way more appealing to your potential employers as well as everybody else if you are well-versed with the technical know-how pertaining to GitHub, a hosting service for the VCS Git. When you happen to share your projects on GitHub, people have access to and are able to see your code, what exactly you happen to be doing, and how you are doing it. GitHub's primary focus is on the proper communication of a variety of ideas that you happen to be working on. Everybody in the tech sector today is making use of Git and/or GitHub in some shape or form.

So, make sure that you at least have a profile on GitHub so that you too can get involved. Additionally, you would also end up with not only a repository but also some commits on your profile page as well. GitHub Pages, furthermore, will be able to host your websites for you. They could be personal websites or sites that are meant for the various projects that you have been involved in. GitHub Pages can be hosted directly from your GitHub repository. You just have to make the necessary edits and follow it up with a push. Your changes, subsequently, will be live. GitHub Pages only give you one site for one account on GitHub, whether you happen to be an individual user or an organization, though you will be allowed to create an unlimited number of project sites or project pages. The User Page is a website with the domain name of http://username.github.io or even http://username.github.com wherein the phrase "username" will be replaced by your GitHub username. The Project Pages mean the websites which are special repositories having the domain name http://username.github.io/myrepo wherein the name of the repository on GitHub is known as myrepo.

Do keep in mind that GitHub Pages is a separate entity not the same as GitHub.

That being said, let's quickly go over all the steps you need to perform to create your own site via GitHub Pages:

- **Creation of a repository:** First head to GitHub and then create a new public repository called username.github.io, where "username" refers to your username, or the name of the organization you are creating a site for, on GitHub. You must remember that if the initial part of the repository does not match your username in an absolutely exact fashion, the process will completely stop working. So, you need to make sure that you get it right.

- **Cloning of the repository:** Now, you shall have to go to the folder where you wish to store your project, as well as clone the new repository. The command to be used here will be ~ $git clone "https://github.com/username/username.github.io."

- **Adding Index File:** This is to be followed up with entering the project folder as well as supplementing it with an index.html file.

- **Committing Changes:** Now, you are supposed to add, commit, and push your changes. The commands for these three, respectively, will be '$git add –all', '$git commit -m "Initial Commit"', and '~$git push -u origin main'.

- **All Done:** You're done now. Make sure that you start a browser and then go to https://username.github.io.

Before beginning your journey on GitHub, there will be a few other aspects that you have got to familiarize yourself with, like:

- **Blogging using Jekyll:** How to use Jekyll to learn to blog, while making use of the beautiful Markdown syntax, a lightweight markup language that helps in the creation of formatted text via the use of a plain-text editor, as well as without having to deal with any particular databases.

- **Custom URLs:** If you wish to use your own customized domain for a site of GitHub Pages, you shall have to create a file called CNAME and include it in your URL as well.

- **Guides:** Familiarize yourself with how to create customized 404 responses for GitHub Pages, the utilization of submodules, and other pertinent details that will help you in better operating this tool.

GitHub Pages is an essential resource that is provided as well as hosted by GitHub. Following are few examples of GitHub Pages:

- The writing of programming books while making use of GitHub as well as Markdown using GitBook. But what is GitBook. GitBook happens to be a command line tool (as well as a Node.js library, meaning an open-source, back-end, cross-platform, JavaScript runtime environment) meant for building beautiful books while making use of GitHub/Git and Markdown (or AsciiDoc, a text document format).

- Turn R Markdown files into Markdown files by making use of Knitr in R-Studio and, subsequently, make an online book. While Markdown is a simple formatting syntax that is utilized for writing Hypertext Markup Language (HTML), PDF, and MS Word documents, R Markdown is a kind of a file format that is utilized for making dynamic documents using R. An R Markdown document would be written in Markdown only, i.e., you will be able to see an easily readable plain text format, but within the text would be embedded chunks of R code.

As mentioned earlier, the purpose of GitHub Pages is simply to allow the GitHub user to create their personal websites as well as sites for projects and repositories. Recently, there also have been a bunch of improvements made on the site of GitHub Pages. Now, whenever someone visits the Pages site, instead of GitHub serving you the content directly, the page gets served by a Content Delivery Network (CDN) that is global in nature, making sure that the nearest physical server should be able to serve a cached page at remarkably high speeds. A cached page is a page that is hidden or stored somewhere within the system, i.e., a short-term memory of the computer where the information gets stored to ensure easy retrieval. A content delivery network, or a content distribution network (CDN), refers to a geographically distributed network of a number of proxy servers (a server application that acts as an intermediary between the client and the resource-provider) as well as their data centers. There has also been another bonus. The GitHub Pages site is now protected through a kind of Denial-of-Service mitigation services that has also been utilized for the site GitHub.com. In computing, a Denial-of-Service attack (short form being DoS attack) is used to refer to a cyberattack where the perpetrator is seeking to make a machine or even a network resource unavailable to the users it is intended for by inducing a temporary or even indefinite disruption in the services of a host that is connected to the Internet. DoS attacks are usually accomplished via a flooding of the targeted resource or machine with a huge number of superfluous requests that will ultimately overload the systems and consequently prevent the legitimate requests, searches, etc., from being fulfilled.

However, if you wish to take advantages of these improved services as a subdomain, custom subdomain, or an A Record with GitHub Pages, you will have to incorporate a few changes:

- **Default Domain:** The default user domain needs to be in the format of username.github.io. Since default subdomains are automatically updated by the Domain Name System (DNS), you don't really need to do anything here.

- **Custom Subdomain:** If you are making use of a custom subdomain (say www.example.com), you will also have to ensure the use of a CNAME record that points at username.github.io.

- **Apex Domain with ALIAS:** If you are currently making use of an A Record, you should be able to tell regarding your need to move if your A Record happens to be pointed at 207.97.227.245 or 204.232.175.78. To check this, make use of the following commands:

```
$ dig example.com
example.com. 7200 IN A 207.97.227.245

OR

$ dig example.com
example.com 7200 IN A 204.232.175.78
```

Some DNS providers, e.g., DNS Simple, will also allow you to use an ALIAS record to be able to point your custom apex domain to username.github.io. A DNS is a decentralized as well as hierarchical naming system for computers, their services, and other resources that are connected to the Internet or some other form of private network. A DNS is able to associate various kinds of information with the domain names assigned to each one of the entities that are participating. Basically, DNS servers shall be able to translate requests for names into particular IP addresses, consequently controlling which server a user shall be able to reach whenever they type a domain name in their web browser. If your DNS provider happens to support this configuration, you will be able to receive the full benefits of not only the CDN but also protection from DoS attacks to your GitHub Pages site. Additionally, if you are able to switch to a subdomain or a DNS provider that will support your ALIAS records, you should also be able to take advantage of the CDN and the DoS mitigation. Lastly, if you happen to be using an apex domain (say example.com) and your DNS provider is not able to support ALIAS records, then the only option at hand that you have is to use A Records for your DNS. This configuration might not give your GitHub Page the benefit of CDN, but it will ensure that you are protected by the DoS mitigation. Do remember to configure your A or ALIAS records.

BASICS OF GITHUB PAGES

You should be able to set up a basic GitHub Pages site for yourself, your organization, or your project, if you familiarize yourself with the basics of GitHub Pages. GitHub Pages is available in the form of public repositories with GitHub Free as well as GitHub Free for Organizations and in the form of public as well as private repositories with

GitHub Team, GitHub Pro, GitHub Enterprise Server, and GitHub Enterprise Cloud.

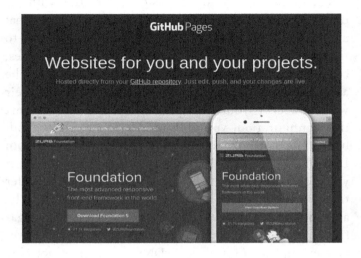

GitHub Pages is a provider for static site hosting services, taking Cascading Style Sheets (CSS), HTML, and JavaScript files, from a repository on GitHub, running the files through a build process (optional), and then publishing them straight as a website. You should also be able to host your site on GitHub's github.io domain or your own customized domain for that matter. If your project site happens to have been published from a private or an internal repository owned by an organization that uses GitHub Enterprise Cloud, you should be able to manage the access control for that same site. The owners of a particular organization can easily disable the publication of a site made using GitHub Pages from that particular organization's repositories.

Since, we mentioned how GitHub Pages is meant for the creation of static sites, we now will be starting a comprehensive detour into the two different kinds of websites, static and dynamic, what the differences between them are, etc.

Static and Dynamic Websites

One might find it difficult to be able to differentiate between a static and a dynamic site, especially with the recent trends turning toward more progressive, as well as hybrid sites and apps, along with an increasing desire for personalization, both from the creators and the consumers. In this section, we will provide a nuanced differentiation between both the kinds of websites, as well as share useful tips and insights that should help you in choosing one of them for the latest project that you wish to undertake.

Static Website

Static websites tend to consist of a fixed number of prerendered web pages, which further contain hard coded as well as fixed structure and content. This is the reason why in a static website, the users will be able to see the exact same content, irrespective of who they happen to be, what browser they use, and what their current location happens to be. Web programmers are usually able to build static website pages by making use of HTML to set up the structure as well as CSS for adding colors and affiliated visual elements. These webpages are generally built independently, without any sort of a connection to an underlying database. Once a static website is published, it shall be staying the same and not reflect any changes due to the action of the user. If you want a change or wish to see something different, you will have to edit the HTML source code manually for each page that is a constituent of the website. This can be tremendously time-consuming as well as a very arduous task, especially if you need to update a particularly large website.

Following are some of the advantages of static websites:

- It takes much less time for static websites to be built as well as deployed if we compare them to the dynamic websites.

- You should be able to duplicate the primary code of a static website to maintain a consistency in elements while also making minor changes for the purposes of differentiation.

- Static sites are way more secure than the dynamic websites.

- It becomes significantly easier for the search engines to be able to rank the static websites because they tend to load significantly faster.

- You shall not be needing a very complex software to build static websites.

- It is cheaper to create a static website rather than a dynamic one.

- You can change the layout as well as the design of every single page in a static website with a fair degree of ease.

- It will be more easy to be able to restore a static website after a Distribution Denial-of-Service (DDoS) attack or a crash through the redeployment of the code base.

There are also a few disadvantages of the static websites:

- If the static website happen to fairly large, the act of making updates can be tremendously challenging as well as time-consuming.

- Once you are done with making the basic structure of the site, it can be tremendously hard to scale it up or add supplementary content.

- Due to the sheer amount of effort that is required to be able to update the static websites, it is very likely that you will end up with stagnant content, making your company as well as brand feel outdated or redundant.

- You will neither be able to interact with your users in any capacity at all nor will be to render them a unique experience.

Dynamic Website

Dynamic websites are able to generate pages for the users in real time. Both the content as well as the structure here is incredibly flexible, making it possible to ensure customization of what a user/visitor will end up experiencing depending on both their request, as well as the browser that they happen to use. If you wish to create a dynamic website, it is imperative that you are well-versed with a server-side programming like C#, Hypertext Preprocessor (PHP), or Python. Unlike static websites, the dynamic websites tend to process their requests as well as pull in their content from either a content management system (CMS) or an external database.

The server-side code that is supposed to be utilized to allow us to build a dynamic website should also be able to generate real-time HTML pages that have been constructed in a manner which fulfills all the individual requests of a user. While the static sites tend to be strictly informational, it is the dynamic websites which contain interactive as well as perpetually changing elements. Consequently, the web developers end up using a combination of server-side as well as client-side programming to be able to create an interactive website experience for their users as well as visitors. Dynamic websites will generate as well as display content based on the actions that have been taken by a user. The degree or the level of change that eventually takes place depends completely on the developer's skill as well as their ability to intricately develop the various interactive elements of a dynamic website. For example, remember the last time you visited your user profile on websites like Walmart or Amazon. Every time you revisit the page, it has been changed, updated with new recommendations based on your past purchase behavior, etc. You are also allowed to pull up information about your past orders or account details in general. This is because these two happen to be dynamic sites that are generating unique user experience for you based on the past actions you have performed on the website or the application.

There are quite a few advantages of the dynamic websites:

- A dynamic website shall give you more website functionality as well as enable good user interaction.

- They allow you to request as well as store information in a highly organized fashion.

- They display their content based on the needs of a user.

- You will be able to get additional website flexibility due to your connection with a CMS.

- Multiple users are allowed to adjust the content as per their desires, wishes, and needs.

- It is significantly less costly for us to make our changes as well as adjustments in a dynamic site when compared to a static site.

- Dynamic sites, statistically speaking, will be able to attract more visitors as well as recurring customers.

The disadvantages of dynamic sites, on the other hand, include the following:

- There are way more functions, you have got to build the site foundation, make connections within the database, and add other features that will hopefully make an effective dynamic website. Unfortunately, the sheer number of these functions makes the development of a dynamic website expensive.

- When it comes to displaying your content on a dynamic website, there are more limitations in terms of design as well as layout.

In early days of the Internet, most of the sites tended to be static sites. So, they were limited to merely displaying content for purposes of either information or entertainment. Since these sites learned nothing as well as knew nothing about the users who were visiting them, it was not possible for web developers to create customized experiences at that point of time.

With the dawn of the Internet Age, users were spending more time on the Internet and were therefore wanting more from their websites. This led the developers to look for ways to make their sites more interactive, allowing for functions like shopping, trading, and real-time interactions with the users. To be able to do this, they had to figure out ways for leveraging their client as well as server-side programming languages and databases to be able to pull real-time content into a particular website.

So, now, you will find that several websites have both static and dynamic web pages. This gives them a lot more flexibility, as far as their layout is concerned, along with the benefits that will be provided to the users, as well as the ability to make changes that will ensure that the content is fresh and is also amenable to getting adapted depending on the changing needs of the users.

The most crucial difference between the static and the dynamic websites is that the content of a static website remains the same until and unless you hire a web developer to change the underlying source code. On the other hand, the information available on a dynamic website gets altered based on a number of factors, like the locations as well as the desires of the users, and even the times of the day when the user seems to be accessing that particular website. Your static content should typically get uploaded accompanied by the web page. What a user will eventually see presented will be the exact same content in the exact same format, irrespective of the actions that they choose to take. On the other hand, as far as the case of dynamic websites is concerned, the content is presented in a plethora of different formats depending on the controls that have been put in place by the site administrators as well as the specific actions performed, say the clicks made, by a user. In case of a static website, it is way easier to cache information, while doing the same for a dynamic website can be slightly more complicated. The content of static sites can easily be stored on, or as technical parlance would refer to it, "cached" on the edge servers of the edge servers of a CDN, letting you have access to the information at significantly higher speeds. As you probably already have heard or experienced, the caching of website content tends to speed up the loading of sites for various users. This is because edge servers tend to get distributed across a number of geographical regions. Consequently, CDNs are able to provide faster as well as more reliable responses for users who are located in the vicinity. But it is simply not practical to do so in the case of dynamic websites because of the sheer number of times that the content tends to change. Apart from that, there are significant security risks that are associated with the storage of a user's personal information.

Another important difference between these two kinds of websites is that the content you see on static sites has come directly from the server only and nowhere else. Dynamic content, on the other hand, will have to pass through a number of application logic layers before it is eventually downloaded from the server. Some of the examples of static content are audio files, images, HTML pages, static online forms, video files, downloads such as spreadsheets, documents, software, etc. And a few examples of dynamic content are user account information, translated web pages, databases, texts, video messaging apps, voice messaging apps, real-time data like stock prices, weather forecasts, data pertaining to the health of individuals, etc.

But how must one go about deciding whether a static or a dynamic site will be the right choice for a particular kind of software development? If your website is to consist of only a few pages, you will be well-advised to prefer a static site. A static website is generally utilized to disseminate information among the people. On the other hand, the information contained by dynamic websites usually is proprietary in nature and therefore only used by entrepreneurs as well as private companies. If as a user, you are logging-in to a dynamic website, you are most probably looking for a piece of restricted information. So if you wish to create a simple blog that is supposed to look great as well as complement your business, it is best that you choose to prefer a static website. Similarly, if you simply require a landing page providing all the basic information about your company, its products, services, etc., go for the development of a static site for this purpose. However, if you wish to develop a good e-commerce site, which will obviously be accompanied by an ever-changing inventory, go for the development of a dynamic website. This should allow you to make recommendations to your users based on the past purchases that they have made from your site. So, if a customer left items in their shopping cart the last time they made a purchase from your site, a dynamic website should be able to conduct functions like prompting the customer to return and complete the purchase that they intended to make initially. A dynamic website should also help you in the creation of progressive web applications (PWA) as well as other applications. So, you must make sure that you base your decision of developing either a static or a dynamic website based on your needs, i.e., what you want the site to provide for you. Utilizing the static website generators can help you if you want your website up and running pretty quickly. Creation of a dynamic website, on the other hand, can be a more complicated process but, accompanied with it, also offers better possibilities for flexibility as well as adaptation as per your needs and requirements.

Types of GitHub Pages Sites

There are three varieties of GitHub Pages sites: project, user, and organization. The project sites are those which are connected to a particular project that was hosted on GitHub, like a recipe collection or a JavaScript library. The user and the organization sites, on the other hand, are supposed to be connected to a specific GitHub account.

For you to be able to publish a user site, you shall have to create a repository that is owned by your user account, named, <username>.github.io. In order for you to publish an organization's site, you shall have to create a repository that is owned by an organization, named, <organization>.github.io. Unless you happen to be making use of a customized domain, the user as well as the organizational sites shall be available at http(s)://<username>.github.io or http(s)://<organization>.github.io.

Additionally, the source files for a specific project site shall be stored in the same repository as the project. Unless you happen to be making use of a customized domain, the project sites should be available at http(s)://<username>. github.io/<repository> or http(s)://<organization>.github. io/<repository>. If you plan to publish your site privately, the URL for the same will be different. Lastly, to reiterate what has previously been mentioned, we are allowed only one user or organization site for each account on GitHub, whereas the project sites, as far as their case is concerned, can be unlimited, whether owned by an organization/ organization account or a user account.

Publication of Sources for GitHub Pages Sites

The source of publication for your GitHub Pages site will be the branch as well as the folder where the source files of the site tend to be stored. However, you must be careful that the GitHub Pages sites will be, by default, publicly available on the Internet. This will hold true even if the repository of this site from an internal or private that might be owned by an organization through the use of GitHub Enterprise Cloud, which usually manages the access control for the site. If the repository of your site contains sensitive data, you will be well advised to remove the said data before going for the final publication.

If the default publishing source happens to exist in your repository, GitHub Pages should automatically be able to publish a site from that source. The default publishing source for the user as well as organization sites happens to be the root of the default branch in the repository. The default publishing source for the project sites tends to be the root of the gh-pages branch. If you wish to keep the source files of your page in a separate location, you shall have to change the publishing source of the site. You will be able to publish the site from any branch in the repository, either from the/docs folder in that branch or the root of the repository on it '/'. If you end up choosing the/docs folder of the branch for the source of your publication, GitHub Pages should be able to read everything so that it can publish your site, along with the CNAME file, from the/docs folder. For example, whenever you shall attempt to edit your customized domain via the GitHub Pages settings, the custom domain shall be writing to the address/docs/CNAME.

Generation of Static Sites

GitHub Pages will be able to publish any kind of a static file that you would push to your repository. You should also be able to create your own static files as well as use static site generator so that it is able to build your site for you. You should also be able to customize your building processes locally or through another server. Here, the best recommendation would be Jekyll, a static site generator that should be able to provide you built-in support for the GitHub Pages alongside a simplified building process. The GitHub Pages make use of Jekyll to allow you to build your site by default. If you want to use a different static site generator, and not Jekyll, you will need to disable the Jekyll build processes via the creation of an empty file called. nojekyll at the root of your publishing source, then subsequently follow the instructions provided by the static site generator of your choice to be able to build your site locally. Keep in mind that GitHub Pages is incompatible with, i.e., is not able to support the server-side languages like PHP, Python, or Ruby.

You also must keep a few guidelines in mind while making use of the GitHub Pages:

- The site GitHub Pages was created after the date of June 15, 2016, and the use of github.io domains was served over HTTPS. If you had created your site before this date, you should be able to enable the HTTPS support for the traffic to your site.

- Your GitHub Pages sites must not also be used for conducting transactions of a sensitive nature, like sending your passwords or your credit card numbers.

- The way you use your GitHub Pages is supposed to be subject to the GitHub Terms of Service, a crucial feature of which is the prohibition on the reselling of sites.

Usage Limits

The GitHub Pages sites must also take care to follow the mentioned usage limits:

- The source repositories of GitHub Pages are to follow a recommended limit of 1 GB.

- The limit for the published GitHub Pages sites is to be no more than 1 GB.

- The sites created by GitHub Pages are provided with a soft bandwidth limit of 100 GB per month. For the uninitiated, a bandwidth limit simply refers to the amount of data that can be transferred from a particular website to a user's computer. So, a website with high traffic would need a lot of bandwidth.

- The GitHub Pages websites are to also follow a soft limit of no more than 10 builds per hour. A soft limit, here, refers to a value that a Linux system makes use of to limit the system's resources for the sake of running processes.

If your site happens to be exceeding these usage quotas, GitHub paged shall not be able to serve your site. You could find yourself receiving an email from GitHub Support that will suggest strategies for reducing the impact of your site on the servers of GitHub Pages. These might include suggestions on putting in place a third-party CDN at the front of your site, as well as utilizing other GitHub features like the releases, or moving to an entirely different hosting service that might be more suitable for your needs.

Prohibition on Usage

GitHub is not supposed to be or allowed to be used like a free web hosting service for the sake of your e-commerce sites, online business, or any other kind of website which is supposed to facilitate your commercial transactions for you or provide you with a commercial software as a service, popularly known by the acronym SaaS. Furthermore, GitHub has mandated that it shall not allow GitHub Pages to be utilized for some certain purposes or activities. Following are some of these prohibited uses of GitHub Pages:

- Any content or activity that is considered illegal or is otherwise prohibited as per the Terms of Service, Community Guidelines, and the Acceptable Use Policies of GitHub.

- Any content or activity that is violent or contains threats.

- Excessive automated mass activities, like spamming.

- Any activity that could potentially compromise GitHub services or its users.

- Any kind of Get-rich-quick schemes.

- Sexually provocative or obscene content.

- Any content that will end up misrepresenting your identity or the purpose of the site.

If you, as a user, have more queries about whether your use or intended use falls into any of the aforementioned categories, you are recommended to contact GitHub Support. Keep in mind that GitHub at all the times reserves the right to reclaim any of the GitHub subdomains without any kind of liability whatsoever.

MIME Types on GitHub Pages

A MIME type is a kind of a header that server would send to a browser, containing information about the nature as well as the format of the kind of files the browser requested for. GitHub Pages can support over 750 MIME types across thousands of file extensions. This list of the supported MIME types is generated using the mime-db project. While you are not allowed to specify the custom MIME types on the basis of each file or repository, you are allowed to add as well as modify the MIME types for your use on the software of GitHub Pages. Let's now briefly delve into the mime-db contributing guidelines.

There is a proper database of all the mime types. A mime consists of a single, as well as public JSON file. JSON (its full form being JavaScript Object Notation) which is a kind of an open standard file format, apart from being a data interchange format as well, that makes use of the human readable text to store as well as transmit the data objects which consist of arrays, as well as the attribute-value pairs. Further, the mime does not include any logic, making it as un-opinionated as it is possible to alongside an Application Programming Interface (API). A mime would also aggregate its data from a variety of sources. The commands for its installation is "npm install mime-db." For the purposes of database download, you need to utilize the JSON file utilizing the methodology of JsDelivr, a free CDN for the open-source software. You are also recommended to replace the master branch with a release tag since it is very likely that the JSON format will get altered in the future. The URL for the same is "https://cdn.jsdelivr.net/gh/jshttp/ mime-db@master/db.json."

Coming to the data structure, the JSON file is supposed to be a map lookup for the lowercase mime types. Each mime has following properties:

- **.source:** This is where the mime type gets defined. If you do not set it, it is probably going to be a custom media type. There are three sub-categories:

  - **apache:** The apache common media types.

  - **iana:** The media types defined by International Assigned Numbers Authority (IANA).

  - **nginx:** The nginx media types.

- **.extensions[]:** The known extensions that are associated with this kind of mime type.

- **.compressible:** Depends on whether a file of this kind can be gzipped.

- **.charset:** The default charset that is associated with this kind, if any.

If unknown, the property can also be mentioned as undefined.

If you wish to be able to edit the database, you only have to make the PRs against src/custom-types.json or src/custom-suffix.jason.

The src/custom-types.json file is a kind of a JSON object with the MIME type as its keys as well as the values being objects with the given keys:

- **compressible:** Leave this out if you don't know it, otherwise try to use true/false so that you are able to indicate whether the data that has been represented by this type can be defined as typically compressible.

- **extensions:** These include a plethora of file extensions that are associated with this type.

- **notes:** The human-readable notes about this type, typically whatever the type seems to be.

- **sources:** These include URLs several in number, where the MIME types as well as their associated extensions are sourced from. It is important that this is a primary source; links to a number of type aggregating sites as well as Wikipedia will simply not be accepted.

For updating the build, you might have to run the command npm run build.

Lastly, let's briefly talk about how you will be able to add the custom media types? The best way for you to acquire the new media types that have been included in this library is through their registration in the International Assigned Numbers Authority (IANA). If you are looking for the community registration process, you will find it comprehensively outlined in the RFC 6838 section 5. The one registered with the IANA shall be automatically pulled into this library. If this doesn't seem possible or feasible for you, these need to be added directly as a custom type. To be able to do this, you will need a primary source that will provide you with a definitive list of the media type. If an extension will be listed as associated with this particular media type, the source will have to definitively link the media type as well as its extension.

In this, we were briefly introduced to GitHub Pages as well as the primary concepts associated with it. Let us move on to the next chapter, where we discuss a range of issues like creating a GitHub Pages site, configuring a publishing source for the GitHub Pages site, changing visibility, cookies, adding a theme, etc. Let us now proceed.

CHAPTER 3

Getting Started with GitHub Pages

IN THIS CHAPTER

➤ Creating GitHub Pages Site

➤ Configuring a Publishing Source for your GitHub Pages Site

➤ Changing the Visibility of your GitHub Pages Sites

➤ Cookies

➤ Adding a Theme

In the previous chapter, we dealt with the two basic issues of what GitHub Pages are, as well as their basics. This chapter has us dealing with a set of issues that have been mentioned previously, namely the creation of the GitHub Pages

DOI: 10.1201/9781003242055-3

site, the configuration of the publishing source for GitHub Pages site, changing visibility of your GitHub Pages sites, the problem of Cookies, adding a theme, etc.

CREATING GITHUB PAGES SITE

Creating a new GitHub Pages site can be done in a new or an existing repository. However, before we delve into this issue, a few things to keep in mind. GitHub Pages can be accessed through public repositories using GitHub Free and GitHub Free for Organizations, as well as in public and private repositories through GitHub Team, GitHub Pro, GitHub Enterprise Server, and GitHub Enterprise Cloud. The owner of organization/organization accounts should be able to restrict the publication of GitHub Pages sites from the repositories that are owned by that particular organization.

Now, coming back to our central concern, if your site happens to be an independent project, you should be able to create a new repository to store the source code of your site. On the other hand, if your site is only associated with a project that already exists, you should be able to add its source code to the repository of that particular project only, in a/docs folder that you should be able to find either on the default branch or a different branch. For example, if you happen to be creating a site for the publication of the documentation of a project that is already present on GitHub, you will have to store the source code for this site in the same repository where your project is. If the account which owns the repository is using either GitHub Free or GitHub Free for Organizations, it is mandatory that the repository be public. If you want to create your site in an existing repository, follow the provided steps:

- Go to your site's repository on GitHub.

- Make the decision on the kind of publishing source that you wish to use.

- If the publishing source of your choice already exists, navigate to it. If it doesn't exist, you shall have to create that source.

- At the root of your publishing source, create a new file with the name "index.md" containing the content that you want to be displayed on the main page of your site.

- Configure the publishing source (Steps provided in a later section).

- Under the repository name, click on the option of Settings.

- In the left sidebar, choose the option "Pages."

- If you happen to be publishing a project site from either a private or an internal repository that is owned by an organization which uses the GitHub Enterprise Cloud, make sure that you choose the visibility that you need for your site. Go to the option "GitHub Pages," and from the "GitHub Pages visibility" drop-down menu, choose your preferred visibility (Optional).

Before you are able to create your own site, you need to have a repository for the same on GitHub. Remember that GitHub Pages sites are publicly accessible online by default, even if your repository happens to be private or internal. If your project site was published from a private or internal repository that was owned by an organization making use of GitHub Enterprise Cloud, you should be able to have some access control for this site. If that is not the case, you are strongly advised to remove any data from your repository that is of sensitive nature, before hitting Publish. Steps to create a repository for your site:

- From the upper-right corner of any page, click on the "+" sign for your drop-down menu and click on the option "New Repository."

- From the "Owner" drop-down menu, select the account that you wish to own the repository.

- Now, type a name for the repository, alongside providing an optional description. If you happen to be creating a user or an organization site, your repository will have to be named <user>.github.io or <organization>.github.io. If the user or the organization name happens to contain uppercase letters, make sure that you lowercase them.

- Choose the kind of visibility that you want for your repository.

- Click on the option "Initialize this repository with a README."

- Lastly, click on the option "Create Repository."

CONFIGURING A PUBLISHING SOURCE FOR YOUR GITHUB PAGES SITE

Before you are able to configure a publishing source, you shall have to make sure that the branch that you want to make use of as a publishing source already exists within your repository. Steps to follow:

- Go to your site's repository on GitHub.

- Click on Settings option under your repository name.

- In the left sidebar, choose the option of Pages.

- Under the option "GitHub Pages," make sure that you use the None or Branch drop-down menu, and subsequently select a publishing source from there.

- Use the drop-down menu to select a folder as your publishing source (Optional).

- Lastly, click on Save.

Managing the Publication of GitHub Pages Site for Your Organization

You should be able to control whether the members of your organization are allowed to publish the GitHub Pages site from the repositories in the organization's account, as well as restrict the visibilities that the members are allowed to choose for the sites. As has been mentioned previously, the owners of an organization are able to manage the publication of various GitHub Pages sites from the repositories of the organization. Additionally, GitHub Pages can be accessed from the public repositories using

GitHub Free as well as GitHub Free for Organizations and from public as well as private repositories, through GitHub Pro, GitHub Enterprise Cloud, GitHub Team, and GitHub Enterprise Server. If your organization is making use of GitHub Enterprise Cloud, you can make a choice on whether to allow organization members to have the facility to create publicly published websites, privately published websites, or both. You are allowed to choose whether you want public publishing or not. If you choose to disallow the publication of the GitHub Pages sites, the sites that have already been published will stay that way. If you want to do so, you can choose to manually unpublish a site. Steps to follow:

- At the top right corner of GitHub, click on your profile photo, then choose the option "Your organizations."

- Right next to the organization, click on "Settings."

- From the left sidebar, press on "Member Privileges."

- Under the option of "Pages Creation," you need to select the visibilities that you wish to allow, as well as deselect the visibilities that you do not need.

- Lastly, click on "Save."

Unpublishing a GitHub Pages Sites

The previous section briefly alluded to how you were allowed to unpublish a GitHub Pages site so that is no longer available. People with maintainer permissions, and obviously, the admins for a repository, are allowed to unpublish a GitHub Pages site.

Unpublishing a Project Site

- Navigate to the main page of your repository on GitHub.

- If you happen to have a gh-pages branch in your repository, make sure that you delete the same. However, if the gh-pages branch happens to be your source, you can skip this as well as the next two steps.

- Under the Repository name, click on Settings.

- From the left sidebar, click on Pages.

- Under the option of GitHub Pages, go to the source drop-down menu and then select None.

- If there happens to be a custom domain that has been enabled for your site, you will have to update your Domain Name System (DNS) settings to avoid a domain takeover.

Similarly, following are the steps for unpublishing a user or an organization site:

- Navigate to the main page of the repository on your GitHub.

- Delete either the branch that you have been using as your publishing source or the entire repository altogether.

- If there happens to be a custom domain that has been enabled for your site, you will have to update your DNS settings to avoid a domain takeover.

CHANGING THE VISIBILITY OF YOUR GITHUB PAGES SITES

You should be able to manage the access control for your project sites by being able to publish that particular site publicly or privately. People who possess the admin permissions for a particular repository should be able to change the visibility of a GitHub Pages site. On GitHub Pages sites, access control is available for private repositories through the use of GitHub Enterprise Cloud. If your project site is being published using an internal or private repository owned by your organization via the use of GitHub Enterprise Cloud, you are still allowed to manage the access control for the site. Using access control, you could choose to publish a site publicly for anybody on the Internet or privately only for the people with the possession of the read access to the repository. A privately published website can be utilized to share the internal knowledge base or the necessary documentation with the fellow members of the organization. You cannot and are not supposed to manage the aspect of access control for any kind of an organizational site. Privately published websites tend to be available at a separate subdomain from the sites that have been published publicly. This makes sure that site you have made using GitHub Pages is secured the moment you hit publish. GitHub Pages automatically secures each subdomain of *.pages.github.io using a Transport Layer Security (TLS) Certificate, as well as ensures the enforcing of HTTP Strict Transport Security (HSTS) so that the browsers are always able to serve the page over Hypertext Transfer Protocol (HTTPS). Not only that, the server also provides a unique subdomain for the private pages to make sure that the other repositories that are owned by your organization are not able to publish their content on the same origin that belongs to the private page. This should be able to protect your private page from a phenomenon called "cookie tossing." We will elaborate on this phenomenon in the next section. This feature of GitHub Pages is the main reason why you would never lose your GitHub Pages sites on the main domain of github.com.

You will also be able to see your site's unique subdomain if you go to the Pages tab of your repository settings. If you use a static site generator that is also configured to develop the site with your repository name as the path, you might have to update the settings for this static site generator when you shall have to change the site to a private mode. If you wish to make use of a more concise as well as memorable domain for a private GitHub Pages site, you are also allowed to configure a custom domain. Steps to change the visibility of your GitHub Pages site:

- Navigate to your site's repository on GitHub.

- Under the repository name, click on the option of "Settings."

- From the left sidebar, click on the option of "Pages."

- From within the subheading "GitHub Pages," access the GitHub Pages Visibility drop-down menu, and then select your choice of visibility.

- Lastly, if you wish to see your published site under the rubric of "GitHub Pages," click the site's URL.

Keep in mind that ideally, it should take up to 20 minutes for the changes that you have made to be incorporated into your site after you have pushed them to the GitHub. If you do not see the new changes incorporated after an hour or so, you might be encountering a case of Jekyll build error, which we shall be talking about in the next chapter.

Securing Your GitHub Pages Site with HTTPS

HTTPS helps in adding a layer of encryption that should prevent others from snooping on you as well as tampering or attempting to adversely affect the traffic of your site. You should be able to enforce HTTPS for your GitHub Pages site to transparently redirect all your HTTP requests to HTTPS instead. People who have the admin permission of a particular repository should be able to enforce HTTPS for their respective GitHub Pages sites.

Regarding HTTPS

All the GitHub Pages sites, as well as the sites that have been properly configured with a custom domain, tend to support HTTPS as well as its enforcement. Nevertheless, it is immensely important to keep in mind that GitHub Pages sites cannot be made use of to carry out transactions of sensitive nature like credit card numbers, passwords, etc.

COOKIES

This section will delve into the phenomenon of cookie attacks or cookie tossing that we briefly alluded to previously. As a software developer, you would sometimes need to perform a migration of your GitHub Pages to their own github.io domain. This sort of a migration can be incredibly important as it helps you with problems like mitigation of the phishing attacks, as well as cookie vulnerabilities that might be spread across domains due to the emergence of practices like hosting customer's content in the subdomain of the main website, etc. In this section, we attempt to look at as well as explore the impact as well as the implications of these cross-domain cookie attacks.

Cookie Tossing in a Subdomain

When you log on to GitHub.com, you will generally set a session cookie by making use of the HTTP headers of your response. This cookie will be containing the session data that will be a unique identifier for you. The session cookies which GitHub tends to send to the web browsers are usually set on the default domain, i.e., github.com. This also means that these cookies are not accessible from any subdomain at *github.com. You shall also have to specify HttpOnly attribute, meaning that you shall not be able to read them if you make use of the document.cookie JavaScript Application Programming Interface (API). Additionally, do make sure that you specify the Secure attribute, meaning that these cookies shall be transferred only via the use of HTTPS. It is the presence of these facilities due to which it is impossible to read or steal the session cookies from a site that is being hosted by GitHub Pages. Session cookies simply cannot be accessed from the jiuser code that is running in GitHub Pages, but due to the working procedure of web browsers with regard to how they send their cookies for the HTTP requests, it gets possible to be able to throw cookies to the GitHub parent domain from a GitHub Pages site. When your browser is performing an HTTP request, it basically sends matching cookies for your URL to a single header called Cookie:, in the form of key-value pairs. Only the cookies which will end up matching the request URL exactly will be sent. For example, you are conducting a request to github.com, a set of cookies for the domain github.io won't be sent, but for. github.com, it will. The cooking tossing issues tend to emanate from a variety of conditions. Sometimes, the header could contain the name as well as the value for every single cookie, but none of the extra information which is required during the setting of the cookies, like the Path or the Domain. A fairly common cookie-tossing attack generally involves the use of the JavaScript API of one cookie for the purpose of setting another cookie on a website hosted by GitHub Pages. Sometimes a website might be hosted under one repository, but the cookie gets sent to all the requests available in the parent domain, even though the cookie was set in a subdomain.

Another instance can be when the cookie set using JavaScript in a subdomain is sent along with the legitimate cookie set that is present in the parent domain, leading to a crisis wherein there is absolutely no way to tell which cookie set seems to be coming from anywhere, considering the fact that the attributes "Domain," "Path," "Secure," "HttpOnly," etc., did not get sent to the server. This can be a major issue for many web servers because RFC 6265 does not provide specific instructions pertaining to the ordering of the cookies that are to be set in domains as well as subdomains. As a consequence, web browsers tend to send them in whatever order they like.

If there happens to be more than one cookie of the same name in the header "Cookie:," the software shall be arbitrarily assuming the first one to be the actual value of the cookie.

There is another highly popular kind of attack. Egor Homakov, a security researcher, wrote about a proof-of-concept attack quite like this one. The state of vulnerability did not end up being too critical since the Cross-Site Request Forgery (CSRF) tokens tend to get reset after each and every single login and thus cannot be permanently fixated. Nevertheless, this example is immensely practical and can help people understand how they should be able to easily reproduce for log out users and subsequently become a major irritant. This often leads to users as well as organizations to migrate from GitHub Pages to their own domain, though your organization will have to ensure that they are well equipped of dealing with the disclosed vector responsible for the attack during the gap period, i.e., when the migration will still be ongoing. A disclosed attack is still not that complicated and should be successfully handled as well as mitigated on the server side. However, this happy certainty might simply not be possible in case of other kinds of attacks that we shall be looking at next.

Protection from Cookie Tossing

The first step of mitigating an attack vector is always the simple act of cookie tossing. To reiterate what was mentioned earlier, an attack of this kind primarily exploits the fact that your web browsers tend to send you two cookie tokens of the same name without really informing you about the domains from which they have actually been set. So, we are simply blindsided about the fact of where each cookie seems to be coming from, and if we also happen to skip the cookie parsing that is provided by Rack, we should be able to see whether a certain request has two duplicate _session cookies. This is because we have somebody attempting to throw cookies from a subdomain, and to deal with this, instead of attempting to guess on our own which key is legitimate and which is simply being tossed, we instruct the web browser to drop the cookie set in our subdomain before proceeding to the regular methodology. To be able to successfully accomplish this, we shall have to craft a very specific response; we will be instructing our web browser to redirect us to the same URL that had earlier been requested, but with a header that is able to drop the subdomain cookie.

```
GET /libgit2/libgit2 HTTP/1.1
Host: github.com
Cookie: logged_in=yes; _session=SESSION_
TOKEN; _session=THIS_IS_A_SESSION_TOKEN;

HTTP/1.1 302 Found
Location: /libgit2/libgit2
Content-Type: text/html
Set-Cookie: _session=; Expires=*day*,
*date* 00:00:01 GMT; Path=/; Domain=.
github.com;
```

Now, we can decide to implement the provided code as a rack middleware. Using this method, the cookie check as well as the subsequent redirect can be easily performed before your application code will be able to run. Whenever the rack middleware will get triggered, the redirect should be able to happen transparently without even the user noticing anything. Now, from here on, your second request will contain only one cookie, the legitimate one. This hack should be adequate to mitigate the straightforward nature of a cookie tossing attack that most people will attempt, but there are other, even more complicated forms of attack, that we shall now deal with briefly.

Cookie Path Workaround

If your malicious cookie is going to have a particular path which is not going to be the root, the web browser should be able to send you that cookie whenever you visit the URL, and whenever you try to clear it in the root path, the header will not make any difference.

```
document.cookie = "_session=SESSION_NAME_
TOKEN; Path=/notifications; Domain=.github.
com"
```

```
GET /notifications HTTP/1.1
Host: github.com
Cookie: logged_in=yes; _session=SESSION_
NAME_TOKEN;
_session=THIS_IS_A_SESSION_TOKEN;
```

```
HTTP/1.1 302 Found
Location: /notifications
Content-Type: text/html
# This header has no effect
Set-Cookie: _session=; Expires=*Day*,
*Date* *Time*; Path=/; Domain=.github.com;
```

The solution for a situation of this kind is pretty straight-forward despite being inelegant; for the request URL, the web browser shall be able to send you a malicious JavaScript cookie if its path happens to match the path of the request URL partially. So, we only need to drop the cookie once for every component of the path.

```
HTTP/1.1 302 Found
Content-Type: text/html
Set-Cookie: _session=; Expires=*day*,
*date* *time*; Path=/; Domain=.github.com;
Set-Cookie: _session=; Expires=*day*,
*date* *time*; Path=/libgit2; Domain=.
github.com;
Set-Cookie: _session=; Expires=*day*,
*date* *time*; Path=/libgit2/libgit2;
Domain=.github.com;
Set-Cookie: _session=; Expires=*day*,
*date* *time*; Path=/libgit2/libgit2/pull;
Domain=.github.com;
Set-Cookie: _session=; Expires=*day*,
*date* *time*; Path=/libgit2/libgit2/
pull/1457; Domain=.github.com;
```

Of course, we are still pretty much blind with regard to the server-side as well as the cookies. An option at hand is the brute-force approach for the sake of clearing the cookies. The method is surely rough but can work very well for your github.io migration.

Cookie Escape

Another attack that can easily be performed is through the use as well as the exploitation of the fact that RFC 6265 does not really specify an escaping behavior for its cookies. So, many web servers and interfaces, like Rack, generally assume that cookie names are allowed to be URL-encoded and therefore should be able to unescape them during the generation of the cookie list. This is a perfectly same assumption to make, especially if your cookie names contain non–American Standard Code for Information Interchange (ASCII) characters.

```
cookies = Utils.parse_query(string, ';,')
{ |s| Rack::Utils.unescape(s) rescue s }
```

This should allow a malicious user to set up a cookie which the web framework can then interpret as _session even though the name of the web browser might not be the same. The attack, then, will only have to escape the characters that do not necessarily have to be escaped.

```
GET / HTTP/1.1
Host: github.com
Cookie: logged_in=yes; _session=chocolate-
cookie; _%73ession=bad-cookie;
{
  "_session" : ["chocolate-cookie",
"bad-cookie"]
}
```

Here, if you end up dropping the second cookie from a list of cookies that your Rack had generated, the header will still have no effect. Crucial information has been lost since Rack's parsing, and the name of the cookie has been

URL-encoded to a separate value from the one that your web framework initially received.

```
# This header has no effect
Set-Cookie: _session=; Expires=*day*,
*date* *time*; Path=/; Domain=.github.com;
```

If we must find our way around this, we will have to skip the Rack's cookie parsing through the disabling of the unescaping and, subsequently, finding the names of all the cookies that should be able to match our targets after we unescape.

```
cookie_pairs = Rack::Utils.parse_
query(cookies, ';,') { |s| s }
  cookie_pairs.each do |k, v|
    if k == '_session' && Array === v
      bad_cookies << k
    elsif k != '_session' && Rack::Utils.
unescape(k) == '_session'
      bad_cookies << k
    end
  end
```

This will allow us to actually drop the right cookie, whether it is our initial one or an escaped variation. If you happen to have this kind of a middleware in place, you should be able to tackle all the cookie tossing attacks which can possibly be tackled on the server side. Next, we will deal with a kind of a vector that can even make your middleware protection useless.

Cookie Overflow

This is an advanced form of the attack that tends to exploit the hard limits of web browsers with regard to the number of cookies that you are allowed to set per domain. For example, for Firefox, this hard limit has been set for up to 150 cookies, while for Chrome, it is 180. The problem here is that the limit has not been defined per cookie Domain attribute but using the actual domain where your cookie had initially been set. One HTTP request to any page of the main domain as well as all its subdomains should be able to send you a maximum number of cookies, though the rules for which ones are to be picked remain undefined. Chrome, for example, simply does not care about the cookies contained within the parent domain, the ones that have been set through HTTP or the ones that have been set as Secure; it simply tends to send the 180 newest ones. What this does is that it makes fairly simple for you to simply "knock out" every single cookie from your parent domain and subsequently replace them with fake cookies, via the use of JavaScript on a subdomain:

```
for (i = 0; i < 100; i++) {
    document.cookie = "cookie" + i +
"=chocolate-chips; Path=/; Domain=.github.
com"
}
```

Once you have managed to set these 180 cookies in your subdomain, all the cookies from your parent domain will just vanish. Now, if we happen to expire the cookies that we had just set, from JavaScript as well, the list of cookies for both the parent domain and the subdomains shall become empty.

```
for (i = 0; i < 100; i++) {
    document.cookie = "cookie" + i +
"=chocolate-chips; Path=/; Domain=.github.
com; Expires=*day*, *date* *time*;"
}
document.cookie = "_session=SESSION_NAME_
TOKEN; Path=/; Domain=.github.com"
```

This should allow you to perform a single request with just one session cookie, the one that has been crafted using JavaScript. The original secure and http only session cookie will now be gone, and subsequently, there will be no way to detect from within the web server is that the cookie that has been sent is neither HttpOnly, Secure, nor set in the parent domain but completely fabricated. If you happened to have sent just one cookie to the server, there is absolutely no way to know whether your cookie is being tossed at all. Even if you happen to detect an invalid key, the very same attack might be used simply to annoy the users by the act of logging them out of GitHub.

So what we observe through the overflowing of cookie jar in the web browser, and we should be able to craft our requests by utilizing cookies that will not be blocked on server-side. As things stand now, if you have been hosting the custom user within a subdomain, that is simply a suicide when it comes to security, and this tends to get exacerbated by the current implementation choices of Chrome. Firefox, on the other hand, is better equipped in handling the distinctions between the parent domain and the subdomain cookies, as it tends to send them for a more rigorous ordering, making sure that their storage is separated to prevent the overflows from any subdomain. Chrome is unable to perform any such distinction and treats the session cookies that have been set using the JavaScript in a similar fashion as the Secure HttpOnly cookies that have been set from the server, creating a potential as well as increasingly enticing ground for the tossing attacks to happen. Irrespective of this the general behavior of cookie transmissions throughout the HTTP headers tends to be so ill-defined as well as dependent upon implementation that is simply a matter of time until someone shows up with a novel way that shall help us toss cookies across domains, irrespective of what our targeted web browser is. Though cookie tossing attacks might not necessarily be critical read pernicious that is they shall not be able to hijack user sessions, or do anything apart from the phishing as well as being an annoyance to the users, it is actually incredibly easy to perform them, and this can prove to be a major problem.

This section focused on the issue of cookie attacks on GitHub Pages, raised awareness on the issue, and emphasized how the difficulties faced for the purposes of protection against these attacks do not necessarily have to entail a full domain migration, which nevertheless remains a drastic but crucial step.

ADDING THEMES

You should be able to add themes to your GitHub pages site so that you are able to customize the look as well as the feel of the site. People who have admin permissions for a particular repository should be able to utilize the theme chooser so that they are able to add a theme to their respective GitHub Pages site.

Theme Chooser

The theme chooser is supposed to add a Jekyll theme to your repository. The working of the theme chooser is entirely dependent on whether your repository is private or public.

- If the GitHub Pages has already been enabled for your repository, the theme chooser should be able to add the theme to the current publishing source.

- If the repository happens to be public, and it is the GitHub Pages that has been disabled for your repository, utilize the theme chooser to enable the GitHub Pages themselves as well as configure the default branch as your publishing source.

- If your repository happens to be private and the GitHub Pages are disabled for your repository, you would have to enable them via configuring a publishing source before you can make use of the theme chooser.

If you have manually added a Jekyll theme to your repository in the past, those files may still be applicable after you are done with your use of the theme chooser.

- **Steps:**
    - Navigate to your site's repository on GitHub.
    - Click on Settings under your repository name.
    - From the left sidebar, click on Pages.

- Click on "Choose a Theme" or "Change Theme" from within the category of "GitHub Pages."

- From the top of the page, choose the theme you want. Subsequently, press on "Select Theme."

- You might also be prompted to edit your site's README.md file. If you want to edit this file later, click on Cancel. Later, you should be able to edit the file by choosing the option "Editing Files."

Your chosen theme will automatically be applicable to the markdown files in your repository. If you wish to apply themes to the HTML files of the repository as well, you shall have to make use of a YAML front matter which might be able to specify a layout for every file.

With this, we have come to the end of Chapter 3. We discussed a range of subjects like the creation of the GitHub Pages site, the configuration of a publishing source, changing the visibility of GitHub Pages sites, the issue of Cookies, adding a theme, etc. We now move to the next chapter, wherein we discuss Jekyll with regard to GitHub Pages, setting up a page, the local testing of a site, the build errors possible, etc. So, let's proceed.

CHAPTER 4

Jekyll and GitHub Pages

IN THIS CHAPTER

➢ Introduction to Jekyll

➢ Installation

➢ Checking your GitHub Pages site locally with Jekyll

➢ Troubleshooting/Build Errors

The previous chapter had us dealing with a variety of issues like the creation of GitHub Pages, the configuration of a publishing source, altering the visibility of your GitHub Pages sites, cookies, and incorporating a theme. In this chapter, we discuss Jekyll, setting up a page using Jekyll, testing a site locally using it, and the build errors which might arise. So, let's begin.

DOI: 10.1201/9781003242055-4

INTRODUCTION TO JEKYLL

Jekyll is the name of a static site generator. It can take text written in a particular markup language and make use of a number of layouts to be able to create a static site. You are also allowed to tweak the site's look as well as feel you, the data that is to be displayed on the page, the URLs to be utilized, etc.

Prerequisites

Jekyll would need the following:

- A Ruby Version that is 2.5 or higher, with all the development headers put in place. You need to check your Ruby Version via the use of ruby-v.

- RubyGems (Here, check your Gems version using gem-v).

- GCC and Make (check for the version through making use of gcc-v, g++ -v, and make -v).

Installation

Jekyll is a Ruby gem that you should be able to install in most of the systems. You can grab it from the homepage https://jekyllrb.com/

Gems are code which you should be able to include in your Ruby projects. Gems package specific functionality within themselves. You should be able to share gems across a number of projects and even with or without people. Gems can perform a variety of functions like:

- Converting your Ruby object to JSON.

- Pagination.

- Interacting with a host of APIs such as GitHub.

Jekyll itself is a gem. Several Jekyll plugins that are available in the market, like jekyll-archives, jekyll-feed, jekyll-seo tag, etc., are also gems. Jekyll can be installed on most of the systems. Now, we will provide you with a detailed set of instructions for all the different operating systems:

- **MacOS:** If you wish to install the command line tools so that you are able to compile your native extensions, you are advised to open a terminal and run the command:

```
xcode-select - -install
```

Setting SDKROOT (only for macOS Catalina or later) – Starting from macOS Catalina (10.15), the headers that are being used for Ruby have had to be moved from their previous location which resulted in some gems like Jekyll failing installation. This issue can be easily resolved through the setting of your SDKROOT in the shell configuration to the value that is provided by xcrun.

Installing Ruby – Jekyll needs Ruby v2.5.0 or later versions. MacOS Big Sur 11.x works well with Ruby 2.6.3. You should be able to verify what version of Ruby you are using through ruby-v. If you happen to have a previous version of macOS, you shall also have to install the newer version of Ruby. Installing with Homebrew can be fairly simple if you intend to use your Ruby for Jekyll. However, if your work involves you switching between various different versions of Ruby, you should prefer to go with a version managers like asdf, rbenv, chruby, rvm, etc.

For Homebrew – To be able to run the latest version of Ruby, you shall have to install it via Homebrew.

- # For the installation of Homebrew

```
/bin/bash -c "$(curl -fsSL https://
raw.githubusercontent.com/Homebrew/
install/HEAD/install.sh)"
```

- # For the installation of Ruby

```
brew install ruby
```

Post this, you must add the brew ruby as well as the gems' path, incorporating it within your shell configuration:

- # If you make use of Zsh

```
echo 'export PATH="/usr/local/
opt/ruby/bin:/usr/local/lib/
ruby/gems/3.0.0/bin:$PATH"' >>
~/.zshrc
```

- # If you make use of Bash

```
echo 'export PATH="/usr/local/opt/
ruby/bin:/usr/local/lib/ruby/
gems/3.0.0/bin:$PATH"' >>
~/.bash_profile
```

- # Unsure about the kind of shell you are using? Type the following command:

```
echo $SHELL
```

If you wish to relaunch your terminal as well as check your setup for Ruby, make use of the following command:

```
which ruby
# /usr/local/opt/ruby/bin/ruby

ruby -v
ruby 3.0.0p0 (2020-12-25 revision
95aff21468)
```

You will now be able to run the latest as well as the most stable version of Jekyll through Ruby.

- **Using rbenv:** Rbenv is generally used because people want to manage several versions of Ruby. Rbenv can be particularly useful if you wish to run a provided

Ruby Version of a project. The required code here would have to be:

- # For the installation of Homebrew

```
/bin/bash -c "$(curl -fsSL https://
raw.githubusercontent.com/Homebrew/
install/HEAD/install.sh)"
```

- # For the installation of rbenv as well as ruby-build

```
brew install rbenv
```

- # For the purposes of setting up rbenv integration using your shell

```
rbenv init
```

- # If you wish to check the installation

```
curl -fsSL https://github.com/rbenv/
rbenv-installer/raw/main/bin/rbenv-
doctor | bash
```

Next, you shall have to restart your terminal so that you are able to apply your changes. This should also allow you to install a specific version of Ruby you are seeking to work on. This is the code for the latest as well as the most stable of Ruby:

```
rbenv install 3.0.0
rbenv global 3.0.0
ruby -v
ruby 3.0.0p0 (2020-12-25 revision
95aff21468)
```

After the installation of Ruby, you shall also have to install Jekyll as well as Bundler.

This has to be followed by the installation of bundler and jekyll gems. The required code for this is:

```
gem install --user-install bundler jekyll
```

You could also acquire a specific Ruby version of your own by using the code:

```
ruby -v
ruby 3.0.0p0 (2020-12-25 revision 95aff21468)
```

Now, you shall also have to append the path of your file, ensuring that you replace n.n with the first two numbers of the Ruby version that you shall be making use of:

- # If you happen to be making use of Zsh

  ```
  echo 'export PATH="$HOME/.gem/ruby/n.n0/bin:$PATH"' >> ~/.zshrc
  ```

- # If you happen to be making use of Bash

  ```
  echo 'export PATH="$HOME/.gem/ruby/X.X.0/bin:$PATH"' >> ~/.bash_profile
  ```

- # If you are unsure of which shell you are using? Type

  ```
  echo $SHELL
  ```

- If you want to check whether GEM PATHS: point toward your home directory:

  ```
  gem env
  ```

Additionally, bear in mind that every single time you shall update your Ruby to a version where the first two digits change, you shall also have to update your path to be able to match the same.

- **Global Install:** We recommend that you do not install Ruby Gems globally so that you are able to avoid any problems pertaining to file permissions as well as the use of sudo.

- **Mojave (10.14):** Because there happen to be SIP Protections in Mojave, you should go with and run the following command on your terminal window:

```
sudo gem install bundler
sudo gem install -n /usr/local/bin/
jekyll
```

- **For Mojave (<10.14):** Here, go for the command:

```
sudo gem install bundler Jekyll
```

TESTING YOUR GITHUB PAGES SITE LOCALLY USING JEKYLL

You should be able to build your GitHub Pages site locally so that you can preview as well as test the changes that have been made to your site. These are the steps to be taken if you want to build your site locally:

- First, open Git Bash.
- Navigate to the publishing source of the site.

- Run bundle install.

- Run the Jekyll site locally using the provided code:

```
$ bundle exec jekyll serve
> Configuration file: /Users/sufyan/
my-site/_config.yml
>              Source: /Users/sufyan/my-site
>         Destination: /Users/sufyan/
my-site/_site
> Incremental build: disabled. Enable
with --incremental
>         Generating...
>                      done in 0.39
seconds.
> Auto-regeneration: enabled for '/
Users/sufyan/my-site'
> Configuration file: /Users/sufyan/
my-site/_config.yml
>    Server address: http://127.0.0.1:4000/
> Server running... press ctrl-c to stop.
```

- If you wish to review your site via your web browser, you shall have to navigate to http://localhost:4000.

TROUBLESHOOTING

It is very likely that you would be running into some problems while you happen to be installing or making use of Git, here are some of the tips that will help you on your journey.

Installation Troubles

If you happen to encounter troubles during a Gem installation, you may feel the need to install some header files so that you are able to compile the extension modules for

Ruby 2.x. You should be able to do this on Ubuntu as well as Debian by running the following command:

```
sudo apt-get install ruby2.6-dev
```

To do the same on CentOS, Red Hat, as well as Fedora Systems, you should go for the command:

```
sudo yum install ruby-devel
```

For Arch Linux:

```
sudo pacman -S ruby-ffi
```

If Ubuntu finds you getting stuck after bundle exec jekyll serve as well as getting error messages like "Could not locate Gemfile" or .bundle/directory, it is highly likely that all the required needs have not been fully met. If you care to notice the recent stock Ubuntu distributions which need the installation of both ruby-all-dev and ruby packages, you should be able to do the same using the following command in your terminal window:

```
sudo apt-get install ruby ruby-all-dev
```

For NearlyFreeSpeech, utilize the provided commands before the installation of Jekyll:

```
export GEM_HOME=/home/private/gems
export GEM_PATH=/home/private/gems:/usr/
local/lib/ruby/gems/1.8/
export PATH=$PATH:/home/private/gems/bin
export RB_USER_INSTALL='true'
```

On Gentoo, you could install the RubyGems by making use of the command:

```
sudo emerge -av dev-ruby/rubygems
```

Windows might require you to install RubyInstaller DevKit.

Make use of the following command for Android Termux:

```
apt update && apt install libffi-dev clang ruby-dev make
```

For macOS, you might have to update RubyGems (make use of sudo only if it is strictly necessary):

```
gem update --system
```

If there are more issues, you shall have to download as well as install new command line interface (CLI) tools like gcc, by making use of the provided command:

```
xcode-select --install
```

This will allow you to install several native gems via the use of the following command (here too, use sudo only if it cannot be helped):

```
gem install jekyll
```

Do make note that the upgradation of macOS might not automatically upgrade your Xcode itself (that shall have to be done separately using the App Store). Additionally, if you happen to have an outdated Xcode.app, it is bound to interfere with the CLI tools that we downloaded earlier. If you happen to face this issue, try upgrading to Xcode as well as install the up-to-date CLI tools.

- **Using Jekyll as a non-superuser (i.e., without sudo):** On many flavors of Bash, macOS, as well as Linux, on Ubuntu, Windows, it is also possible to make use of Jekyll being a non-superuser as well as without using any gems for system-wide locations by adding the provided lines at the end of your .bashrc code file:

```
# Ruby exporting
export GEM_HOME=$HOME/gems
export PATH=$HOME/gems/bin:$PATH
```

This command shall be able to tell gem that it's gems should be placed within the home folder of the user, and not necessarily in a location stretching throughout the system, apart from being able to add the local jekyll command to the user PATH before any of the system-wide paths.

This can prove to be incredibly helpful if you make extensive use of shared web hosting services, wherein only limited privileges are bestowed upon the user accounts. If you add all of these exports to .bashnrc before going for the command gem install jekyll bundler, you will initiate a non-sudo install of Jekyll.

If you wish to activate the new exports, you must either close and restart bash, followed by the logout and login of your shell account. Alternatively, you should be able to run. bashnrc in the presently running shell.

Next, if you come across the following error while you are running the jekyll new command, the aforementioned process will again be useful in resolving the crisis at hand.

- **jekyll new test:** To run bundle install in /home/user/test...

    Your user account not being permitted to install to the system RubyGems.

    You should be able to cancel the installation as well as run:

    ```
    bundle install --path vendor/bundle
    ```

    if you desire to install the gems into ./vendor/bundle/, or you should be able to enter your password as well as install the bundled gems into the RubyGems using sudo.

- **Password:** Once you are done with this, the command jekyll new should be able to work properly for your user account.

- **Jekyll and macOS:** Ever since the System Integrity Protection has been introduced in v10.11, many directories that were considered writable earlier are now mere system locations and available no more. Considering these changes, you should still have a couple of simple ways to get up and running. One of these options is to change your location where your gem is supposed to be installed (here again, you must make use of sudo if you deem it necessary):

```
gem install -n /usr/local/bin jekyll
```

Alternatively, Homebrew should be installed as well as used to set up Ruby. This can be achieved by typing out the provided code:

```
ruby -e "$(curl -fsSL https://raw.
githubusercontent.com/Homebrew/install/
master/install)"
```

If your Homebrew has been installed, the second step is to run the following command:

```
 brew install ruby
```

If you happen to be an advanced user with highly complex needs, you might also find it handy to go for one of the several version managers available for the purposes of installing Jekyll, like rbenv, RVM, chruby, etc.

If you are making use of one of the aforementioned ways to be able to install Ruby, you must make sure that you modify your $PATH variable by making use of the following command:

```
export PATH=/usr/local/bin:$PATH
```

Graphical User Interface (GUI) should also be able to modify your path in an effective fashion if you make use of the command:

```
launchctl setenv PATH "/usr/local/bin:$PATH"
```

GUI apps should also be able to modify your $PATH in the following fashion:

```
launchctl setenv PATH "/usr/local/bin:$PATH"
```

Either of these provided strategies could prove to be tremendously useful since the address /usr/local is known to be a "safe" location on the systems that are SIP enabled, avoiding conflicts with the Ruby version which is included by Apple, keeping Jekyll as well as its dependencies in a sandboxed environment. There is also an additional benefit of not really needing sudo if and when you wish to add or remove a particular gem.

Unable to Find a JavaScript Runtime

This error can emerge when you happen to be installing jekyll-coffeescript while not having a decent JavaScript runtime. To resolve the issue at hand, either install execjs as well as therubyracer gems or install nodejs.

Problems while Running Jekyll
macOSPermalink
Jekyll is compatible with macOS of ARM64 architecture. Nevertheless, bundle exec jekyll serve might fail with the older version ffi.

You might also have to run the bundle update as well as update your ffi to at least 1.14.2 manually.

Debian/Ubuntu
On Ubuntu as well as Debian, you shall have to add /var/lib/gems/1.8/bin/ in your path if you wish to have the jekyll executable be available in your Terminal window.

Base-URL Problems
Let us say you are using a Base-url option like:

- jekyll serve --baseurl '/blog'

...then you must also make sure that you access this site at:

- http://localhost:4000/blog/index.html

Keep in mind that, it WON'T if you just use

- http://localhost:4000/blog

Updating the Gems for Your GitHub Pages

Jekyll happens to be an open source project that gets updated frequently. If the gem of github-pages that is on your system happens to become out-of-date with the gem of GitHub pages on your server, your site might be looking different when it is actually published than when it was being built locally. If you want to avoid this, you must make sure that you regularly update the gem of github-pages on your system. Steps:

- First, open the Git Bash.

- Update the gem of github-pages. If you have Bundler installed within your system, go for the command bundle update github-pages. Otherwise, run the command gem update github-pages.

Configuration Problems

There is a mandated order of precedence if you wish to deal with conflicting configuration settings, which is provided below:

- Command-line flags

- Configuration file settings

- Defaults

This is to say, your defaults will be overridden by the options that have been prespecified in the _config.yml as well as the flags that have been specified at command-line need to override all the other settings that have been specified elsewhere. Additionally, make note that from v3.3.0 onward, Jekyll will not be able to process node_modules as well as some of the subdirectories within the vendor, by default. But became it has an exclude: the array is defined explicitly within the config file overriding its default settings, which might result in the users encountering errors during the construction of the site, with this message being displayed:

- ERROR: YOUR SITE COULD NOT BE BUILT:

```
-------------------------------------
    Invalid date '<%= Time.now.
strftime('%Y-%m-%d %H:%M:%S %z') %>':
    Document 'vendor/bundle/gems/
jekyll-3.4.3/lib/site_template/_
posts/0000-00-00-welcome-to-jekyll.
markdown.erb'
    does not have a valid date in front
matter.
```

If you are adding vendor/bundle to the exclude: list, it should be able to solve this particular problem, but it would also lead to the creation of other sub-directories under /vendor/ as well as /node_modules/, if present, will also be processed to the destination folder _site.

The proper solution involves the incorporation of the default setting for exclude: rather than attempting to override it completely.

So, for the versions up to v3.4.3, the exclude: setting must look like this:

```
exclude:
   - Gemfile
   - Gemfile.lock
   - node_modules
   - vendor/bundle/
   - vendor/cache/
   - vendor/gems/
   - vendor/ruby/
   - any_additional_item # any additional
user-specific listing goes at the end
```

From v3.5 onward, Gemfile and Gemfile.lock are excluded by the default settings. So, in most of the situations, you do not need to define yet another exclude: array within the config file. So an existing definition needs to be modified or eliminated, or commented on so that you could do easy edits in all your future projects.

Markup Problems

Jekyll tends to use various markup engines, and it might have some issues with a few of them. Let's delve into some of them.

- **Liquid:** Liquid 2.0 breaks the use of {{ as far as the use of templates is concerned. Unlike in the older versions, the use of {{ in 2.0 is likely to trigger the mentioned error:

  ```
  '{{' was not properly terminated with
  regexp: /\}\}/  (Liquid::SyntaxError)
  ```

- **Excerpts:** Ever since v1.0.0, Jekyll has utilized automatically generated post excerpts. Jekyll also makes sure that it passes these excerpts through Liquid, which might trigger serious errors wherein the references cease to exist or tag just does not get closed. If you come across errors of this kind, set excerpt_separator: " " in the _config.yml, or try setting it to a different nonsense string.

- **Production Problems:** If you happen to run into an issue wherein a static file refuses to be found within the production environment during the build ever since v3.2.0, it is imperative that you set your environment to "production." This issue tends to be generally caused by attempting to copy a non-existent symlink.

This chapter focused on Jekyll, how one could set up GitHub Pages using it, testing your site locally, delving into a variety of build errors, etc. The next chapter will have us moving on to the topic of custom domains, what they are, how to manage a custom domain, troubleshooting needed, etc. So, let's proceed.

CHAPTER 5

Configuring a Custom Domain

IN THIS CHAPTER

➢ What is a Custom Domain?

➢ Managing a Custom Domain for GitHub Pages Site

➢ Troubleshooting Custom Domains and GitHub Pages

You are allowed to customize the domain name for your GitHub Pages site.

WHAT IS A CUSTOM DOMAIN?

A custom domain is supposed to be a unique branded name that helps in the identification of a particular website. For example, Google's custom domain is google.com. Custom domains are also referred to as Vanity URLs since they appear in the address bar at the top of the browser. They

DOI: 10.1201/9781003242055-5

are made use of prolifically as well as every day because they help users in navigation around the world wide web (www). You probably have many of your favorite as well as frequently used domains bookmarked or memorized. However, the way people understand custom domains is very different from the way computers understand them. Devices like phones and computers that make use of networks do not use letters and words to communicate like you and I do. Instead, they make use of numbers and codes. Thankfully, the www has instituted a system that ensures the translation of a domain name that we type within our browser to the Internet Protocol (IP) addresses that the systems make use of, so that they can identify themselves on networks. This system is known as a Domain Name System, or DNS. DNS is the system which allows for branded and custom domains to get attached to various websites.

Features of a Domain

A domain will be able to give you two powerful features: your own web address and an opportunity to be able to create your custom domain email addresses. Your domain registrar should be able to offer you email services as well as web hosting apart from making sure that your email and your domain name gets properly registered. You wouldn't even have to worry about the payment for web hosting, in most of the cases. Your web address would generally include your root domain as in example.com, your www domain as in www.example.com, and subdomains as in word.example.com. Most of your websites are set up in such a fashion that if you shall type example.com in your browser, the system will be redirecting you toward www.

example.com. The phrase "www" is added for you from the browser's side. This is a technical process meant to connect the root domain with the www domain, which also involves the creation of an HTTP redirect within your DNS records.

GitHub supports the use of custom domains, as well as changing the root of the site's URL from the default domain, like OctoCat.github.io to any other domain of your own choice.

Supported Custom Domains

You should be able to operate GitHub Pages with two separate kinds of domains: subdomains and apex domains. To provide examples, an example of www subdomain is www.name.com, for a custom subdomain, it would have to be blog.name.com, and for apex domain, it shall have to be name.com. You must be able to set up either apex or www subdomain configurations for your website or both of them. It is recommended that you always make use of a www subdomain, even if you happen to own an apex domain. When you create a new site using an apex domain, the software will automatically attempt to secure your www subdomain for your use when it is supposed to serve the content of your site. If you have already configured a www subdomain, we shall be automatically attempting to secure your associated apex domain.

After you are able to configure a custom domain for your user or your organization site, the custom domain shall be replacing the <user>.github.io or <organization>.github.io portion of URL for any of the project sites that are owned by the account and do not happen to have their custom domain configured. So if the custom domain of your user site happens to be www.octocat.com, and your project site published from a repository called octo-project does not have a configured custom domain, the GitHub Pages site for your repository should still be available at octocat.com/octo-project.

Use of a Subdomain for Your GitHub Pages Site

A subdomain is supposed to be a part of a URL before even the root domain. You should be able to configure your subdomain as www or even as a distinct section of your site, like blog.name.com. Subdomains are configured through the use of a CNAME record via your DNS provider.

www Subdomains

A www subdomain is the most common type of subdomain. For example, www.name.com happens to be a www subdomain. These subdomains tend to be the most stable since www subdomains are never affected by the changes that are made to the IP addresses of the servers of GitHub.

Custom Subdomains

A custom subdomain happens to be a kind of a subdomain that does not make use of the standard www variant. Custom subdomains tend to be mostly used when you seek two separate sections of your site. For example, you should try creating a site named blog.name.com and later customize this section independently of www.name.com.

Using Apex Domains for Your GitHub Pages Site

An apex domain tends to be a custom domain that has no subdomain, like name.com. Apex domains are also referred to as bare, base, naked, zone apex, or root apex domains.

An apex domain is configured using the records A, ALIAS, and ANAME via your DNS Provider. If you happen to be using an apex domain as your custom domain, it is highly recommended you set up a www subdomain. If you are able to configure the accurate records for every domain type via your DNS recorder, GitHub Pages should automatically be able to create redirects across domains. So, if you are trying to configure www.name.com for being the custom domain of your site, and you also happen to have the DNS for GitHub Pages, along with its records set up for apex as well as www domains, then name.com shall be able to redirect you to www.name.com. Do keep in mind that the automatic redirects apply only to the subdomain www. Automatic redirects will not be applicable to any other subdomain, like blog.

Updating Custom Domains When Your GitHub Pages Site Gets Disabled

If your GitHub Pages site has become disabled but happens to have a custom domain set up, you will have to immediately update or remove your DNS records contained within your DNS Provider to avoid the risk of a domain takeover. If your custom domain is configured through your DNS Provider while your site itself happens to be disabled, you might have a situation with someone else hosting their site on one of the subdomains that belong to you. There are more reasons regarding why your site might get disabled:

- If you happen to downgrade from GitHub Pro to GitHub Free, any of the GitHub Pages sites that were published from the private repositories of your account shall get unpublished.

- If you happen to transfer a private repository to a personal account via the use of GitHub Free, that repository will lose its access to GitHub Pages feature, and the site that is currently in publication shall get unpublished.

MANAGING A CUSTOM DOMAIN FOR GITHUB PAGES SITE

You should be able to set up and update your DNS records as well as your repository settings to be able to point to the default domain of your GitHub Pages site toward a particular custom domain. People who have the admin permissions for the repository of a GitHub Pages site should be able to configure a custom domain for it.

You will have to make sure that you add the custom domain for your GitHub Pages site before you are able to configure your custom domain through the utilization of your DNS Provider. If you configure your custom domain through your DNS Provider without adding the same custom domain to GitHub, it could potentially lead to someone else getting to host their site on one of the subdomains that belong to you. Do keep in mind that these DNS changes sometimes take up to 24 hours to get incorporated.

Configuring a Subdomain

If you wish to setup a custom domain or a www, like www. name.com or blog.name.com, you shall have to add the domain in your repository settings, which should be able to create a CNAME file for the repository of your website. Post this, you should be able to configure your DNS Providers' CNAME record.

- Navigate to your site's repository on GitHub.

- Choose the option of "Settings" under your repository name.

- Click on "Pages" from the left sidebar.

- Type your custom domain under the option of "Custom Domain," then choose "Save." This should be able to create a commit that would add a CNAME file to your publishing source's route.

- Post this, you will have to navigate to your DNS Provider and subsequently create a CNAME record that should be able to point toward your subdomain within the default domain of your website. So, if you wish to use the subdomain www.name.com during the creation of your user site, you will have to create a CNAME record that should pinpoint www.name.com toward <organization>.github.io. The CNAME record is always supposed to point toward either <organization>.github.io or <user>.github.io, barring the repository name. However, it is strongly recommended to you to not use wildcard DNS records, like *.name.com. A wildcard DNS should allow pretty much anyone to be able to utilize one of your subdomains to host a GitHub Pages site.

- Open your terminal.

- To confirm that your DNS record has been configured correctly, make use of the dig command and replace www.name.com with the name of your subdomain in your code.

```
$ dig WWW.NAME.COM +nostats +nocomments
+nocmd
    > ;WWW.NAME.COM.
IN     A
    > WWW.NAME.COM.                    3592
IN        CNAME   YOUR-USERNAME.github.
io.
    > YOUR-USERNAME.github.io.
43192   IN        CNAME
GITHUB-PAGES-SERVER.
    > GITHUB-PAGES-SERVER.             22
IN     A         192.0.2.1
```

- Unless you happen to use a static site generator for the sake of the local development of your site as well as to be able to push these generated files to your GitHub, make sure that you also pull the commit that had added the CNAME file into your local repository.

- Additionally, if you want to enforce an HTTPS encryption for your website, you shall have to choose Enforce HTTPS. However, it might take up to 24 hours before this option will be available at your disposal.

Configuring an Apex Domain

If you need to set up an apex domain like name.com, you shall have to configure a CNAME file from your GitHub Pages repository and at least one ALIAS, A, or ANAME record that must also be accompanied by a DNS Provider. So, if you happen to use an apex domain for your custom domain, it is highly recommended that you also set up a www subdomain. So, if you are able to configure the correct records for every domain type via your DNS Provider, GitHub Pages should automatically be able to create redirects across domains. So, for example, if you have configured www.name.com as a custom domain for your website, and you also have the DNS records for GitHub Pages set up for www as well as apex domains, then rest assured that name.com shall be able to redirect you to www.name.com. However, do note down that the automatic redirects can only be applied to the www subdomain. Therefore, for other subdomains like blog, automatic redirects will not be applicable.

- Navigate to your site's repository on GitHub.

- Choose the option of "Settings" under your repository name.

- Click on "Pages" from the left sidebar.

- Type your custom domain under the option of "Custom Domain," then choose "Save." This should be able to create a commit that would add a CNAME file to your publishing source's route.

- Now, you shall have to navigate toward your DNS Provider and follow it up with creating either an A, ANAME, or ALIAS record. You should also be able to create your AAA records for support in IPv6. To acquire more information on how to create the right record, check for the documents by your DNS

Provider. If you wish to create an ANAME or ALIAS record, point the apex domain toward the default domain for your website. For the sake of creating A records, however, you shall have to find the apex domain of your site and, subsequently, point it toward the IP addresses for various GitHub Pages.

- 185.199.108.152

- 185.199.109.152

- 185.199.110.152

- 185.199.111.152

Lastly, if you need to create the AAAA records, point the apex domain of your GitHub pages toward the IP addresses.

- 2606:50c0:8000::152

- 2606:50c0:8001::152

- 2606:50c0:8002::152

- 2606:50c0:8003::152

However, as mentioned in the previous section as well, it is strongly recommended that you do not use the wildcard DNS records like *.example.com. Doing this will lead to the dangerous proposition of anyone being able to host a GitHub Pages site on one of the subdomains that belong to you.

- Open the Terminal Git Bash.

- If you need to confirm that your DNS record has been configured correctly, make use of the dig command. Do make sure that you replace *NAME.COM* with the name of your apex domain. Additionally, ensure confirming that the results you end up with match the IP addresses that have been provided for the GitHub Pages above.

- For A records

  - $ dig *NAME.COM* +noall +answer -t A

  - > *NAME.COM* 3600 IN A 185.199.108.152

  - > *NAME.COM* 3600 IN A 185.199.109.152

  - > *NAME.COM* 3600 IN A 185.199.110.152

  - > *NAME.COM* 3600 IN A 185.199.111.152

- For AAAA records

  - $ dig *NAME.COM* +noall +answer -t AAAA

  - > *NAME.COM*   3600   IN AAAA 2606:50c0:8000::152

  - > *NAME.COM*   3600   IN AAAA 2606:50c0:8001::152

  - > *NAME.COM*   3600   IN AAAA 2606:50c0:8002::152

  - > *EXAMPLE.COM* 3600   IN AAAA 2606:50c0:8003::152

- If you happen to use a static site generator for the sake of the local development of your site as well as to be able to push these generated files to your GitHub, make sure that you also pull the commit that had added the CNAME file into your local repository.

- Additionally, if you want to enforce an HTTPS encryption for your website, you shall have to choose Enforce HTTPS. However, it might take up to 24 hours before this option will be available at your disposal.

Configuring an Apex Domain as well as the www Subdomain Variant

While using the apex domain, it is highly recommended that you configure your GitHub Pages site, for you to be able to host content at apex domain as well as the www subdomain variant of that particular domain. To be able to setup a www subdomain along with the apex domain, you will need to configure an apex domain, that should be able to create A, ANAME, or ALIAS records with your DNS Provider. After your apex domain is configured, you would also have to configure your DNS Provider's CNAME record.

- First, you will have to navigate toward your DNS Provider and follow it up by creating a CNAME record that is able to point your site www.name.com toward its default domain <organization>.github.io or <user>.github.io. Make sure that you do not mention the name of the repository. If you need more information on how you should go about creating the correct record, go check out the documentation of your DNS Provider.

- If you wish to confirm that your DNS record has been configured rightly, make use of the dig command, replacing *WWW.NAME.COM* with the name of your www subdomain variant.

```
$ dig WWW.NAME.COM +nostats +nocomments
+nocmd
    > ;WWW.NAME.COM.                        IN
A
    > WWW.NAME.COM.             3592    IN
CNAME    YOUR-USERNAME.github.io.
    > YOUR-USERNAME.github.io.       43192
IN      CNAME    GITHUB-PAGES-SERVER.
>   GITHUB-PAGES-SERVER.          22      IN
A       192.0.2.1
```

Eliminating a Custom Domain

To be able to remove a particular custom domain, follow the provided procedure:

- Navigate to your site's repository on GitHub.

- Choose the option of "Settings" under your repository name.

- Click on "Pages" from the left sidebar.

- Under the option of "Custom Domain," press on "Remove."

TROUBLESHOOTING CUSTOM DOMAINS AS WELL AS GITHUB PAGES

You should be able to check to find common errors to resolve the issues pertaining to custom domains or even the HTTPS of your GitHub Pages site. In this section, we will discuss a plethora of issues like CNAME errors, DNS misconfiguration, HTTPS errors, unsupported custom domain names, browser cache, and URL formatting on Linux.

CNAME Errors

Custom domains are generally stored in a CNAME file at the root of the publishing source. You should be able to add as well as update this file via your repository settings or even manually. If you want your site to render at the right domain, you must ensure that your CNAME file continues to exist in the repository. For example, several static site generators end up force pushing to your repository, which tends to overwrite the CNAME file that had been added in your repository when you had first configured your custom domain. If you generally develop your site locally as well as push your generated files into GitHub, you must make sure that you also pull the commit that had first added the CNAME file to your local repository, so that that file itself gets included in the build. Then, ensure that your CNAME file is also named and formatted correctly.

- The domain name has to be unique throughout all the GitHub Pages sites. So, if we already have a CNAME file called name.com in a particular repository, you shall not be allowed to use the filename name.com even for a file in a different repository.

- The CNAME file needs to contain the domain name only. For example, www.name.com, name.com, or blog.name.com should suffice perfectly.

- The CNAME file must not contain more than one domain. If you wish to pinpoint toward multiple domains in your site, you need to set up a redirect via your DNS Provider.

- The filename must all be in uppercase.

DNS Misconfiguration

If you are not able to point the default domain of your site toward your custom domain, you shall have to contact your DNS Provider. You can also use one of the given two methods to check whether the DNS records of your custom domains have been configured properly:

- A DNS lookup tool that will be easily available online.

- A CLI tool like dig.

- Custom domain names that happen to be unsupported

If your custom domain name happens to be unsupported, you should have to change the status of your domain to a supported one. You would also have to contact your DNS service provider and see if they are willing to offer you forwarding services for your domain names. Also, make sure that your sites do not:

- Use any more than one apex domain. For example, both name.com and anothername.com.

- Use any more than one www subdomain. For example, the use of both name.com and anothername. com.

- Simultaneous use of apex domain as well as custom subdomain. For example, both name.com and docs. name.com.

However, the www subdomain is the one and the only exception. If it has been configured correctly, the www subdomain should be able to automatically redirect you toward the apex domain.

HTTPS Errors

GitHub Pages sites makes use of custom domains that are configured using the records CNAME, ALIAS, ANAME, or A DNS records that can be accessed over HTTPS. It might sometimes take around an hour for the site to become active via https after you are able to configure your custom domain. After updating your DNS settings, you might also have to remove as well as re-add the custom domain of your site repository to initiate the process of the enabling of HTTPS. If you happen to be making use of the CAA records, i.e., the Certification Authority Authorization records, make sure that at least one of your CAA records exists holding the value letsencrypt.org, so that your site can be accessed via HTTPS.

URL Formatting on Linux

If your site's URL happens to contain an organizational name or a username containing dashes, i.e., a name that starts or ends with a dash, or even something that contains consecutive dashes, people who will be browsing via Linux shall be able to receive a server error if and when they attempt to visit your website. To be able to fix this, you need to change your GitHub username so that you can remove non-alphanumeric characters from it.

Browser Cache

If you have changed your custom domain recently or removed it altogether, and find yourself unable to access the new URL of your browser, you might have to clear your browser's cache so that you are able to receive the new URL address. If you happen to be curious about the exact procedure of clearing your cache, you need to go and check out your browser's documents.

Appendix

A BRIEF CHEATSHEET

Git is a VCS that will let you manage as well as keep track of your source code history (known as SCM – Source Code Management).

GitHub, additionally, happens to be a cloud-based hosting service that will let you manage Git Repositories. If you happen to have open-source projects that make use of Git, then GitHub is supposed to design to help you in managing them better.

- Important Commands and Functions:

    - **git init:** This will create a .git repository in your project.

    - **git add:** This will add everything from the project folder to the staging area.

    - **git add*.html:** This would add all your .html files to the staging area.

    - **git add filename.extension:** Replace "filename. extension" to the file you want to add like "index. html."

- **git status:** This will show us what has already been added to the staging area and which files have been altered, and need to be moved to the staging area.

- **git commit -m "Description":** This will take the files present in your staging area and subsequently commit them to the local repository. You would have to describe your commit in brief details like "fixed bug because the user name wasn't getting updated."

- **git branch <branch-name>:** It should be able to create a new branch.

- **git checkout <branch-name>:** This command is supposed to be used for switching the branch.

- **git push origin <branch-name>:** This should be able to push your local repository to your remote repository.

- **git clone <repo-url>:** If you do not have your project on your system, this should allow you to clone the project within the directory you are working with.

- **git pull <remote> <branchname>:** If you are supposed to be working on the same codebase with other people, this command should allow you to pull the latest version from a remote repository and update the local version.

- **git config:** global user.name "Name" git config – global user.email "Email" – This should be able to set up your information that is to be utilized every time you shall be conducting a commit. This would only have to be done one time when you install Git.

Advantages of Using GitHub Pages for Purposes of Hosting

You do not have to be a web developer to learn how to set up a website using GitHub Pages. If you wish to create a portfolio and host it on a site where everyone interested in taking a look at your work can access it, GitHub pages can prove to be an incredibly useful tool. Some of the advantages of using GitHub pages for websites are provided below:

- **Making Public Repo:** It is obvious that you wouldn't want to spend a tremendous amount of money while you are only setting up your first website. It is probably going to be a half experimentation project wherein a free hosting service has encouraged you to get started. Of course, the only important thing to remember is that the repo as well as the code have to be kept public.

- **Supporting Custom Domain:** GitHub Pages is accompanied by the default domain name which goes like: https://<account_name>.github.io/. GitHub also allows you to use your own name, after you have set up your custom domain, of course. The setup takes a couple of days, after which you should be able to use your domain like a pro.

- **Supporting HTTPS:** The primary purpose of HTTPS is encryption. After setting up your custom domain, acquire an SSL certificate and choose the Enforce HTTPS option.

- **Jekyll installation not paramount:** It is not necessary for you to get Jekyll installed within your system even if your site itself was developed using Jekyll. Jekyll, here, is a parsing engine bundled as a ruby gem utilized for the development of static sites from a number of dynamic components, like templates, liquid codes, markdown, partials, etc. In simpler terms, it is supposed to be a simple as well as blog aware static website generator.

- **Pushing to Repo:** GitHub would be able to build your website for you every time you push to a repo called <username>.github.io as long as you have the files required by Jekyll, like _configure.yml _layouts/ default.html and others.

If you happen to be an experienced GitHub user and are comfortable using Git, you would appreciate the contributions version control makes to your work. You can make a change, commit it, and roll back if do not like the results.

Index